PENTECOST 3

Interpreting the Lessons of the Church Year

William L. Holladay

PENTECOST 3

PROCLAMATION 6 | SERIES C

FORTRESS PRESS | MINNEAPOLIS

PROCLAMATION 6
Interpreting the Lessons of the Church Year
Series C, Pentecost 3

Copyright © 1997 Augsburg Fortress. All rights reserved. Except for brief quotations in critical articles or reviews, no part of this book may be reproduced in any manner without prior written permission of the publisher. Write to: Augsburg Fortress, Box 1209, Minneapolis, MN 55440.

Scripture quotations, unless otherwise indicated, are from the New Revised Standard Version Bible, copyright © 1989 by the Division of Christian Education of the National Council of Churches in the U.S.A. and are used by permission.

Cover design: Ellen Maly
Text design: David Lott

The Library of Congress has cataloged the first four volumes of Series A as follows:

Proclamation 6, Series A: interpreting the lessons of the church
   year.
      p.   cm.
   Contents: [1] Advent/Christmas / J. Christiaan Beker — [2] Epiphany / Susan K. Hedahl — [3] Lent / Peter J. Gomes — [4] Holy Week / Robin Scroggs.
   ISBN 0-8006-4207-4 (v. 1 : alk. paper) — ISBN 0-8006-4208-2 (v. 2 : alk. paper) — ISBN 0-8006-4209-0 (v. 3 : alk. paper) — ISBN 0-8006-4210-4 (v. 4 : alk. paper).
   1. Bible—Homiletical use. 2. Bible—liturgical lessons, English.
   BS534.5P74 1995
   251—dc20   95-4622
                                                                                       CIP
   Series C:
   Advent/Christmas / E. Elizabeth Johnson—ISBN 0-8006-4231-7
   Epiphany / Richard I. Pervo—ISBN 0-8006-4232-5
   Lent / Bernhard W. Anderson —ISBN 0-8006-4233-3
   Holy Week / Patricia Wilson-Kastner—ISBN 0-8006-4234-1
   Easter / L. William Countryman—ISBN 0-8006-4235-X
   Pentecost 1 / Terence E. Fretheim—ISBN 0-8006-4236-8
   Pentecost 2 / James L. Boyce—ISBN 0-8006-4237-6
   Pentecost 3 / William L. Holladay—ISBN 0-8006-4238-4

The paper used in this publication meets the minimum requirements of American National Standard for Information Sciences—Permanence of Paper for Printed Library Materials, ANSI Z329.48-1948.

Manufactured in the U. S. A.   AF 1-4238

01   00   99   98   97   1   2   3   4   5   6   7   8   9   1

Contents

Twentieth Sunday after Pentecost   7
Twenty-Seventh Sunday in Ordinary Time/Proper 22

Twenty-First Sunday after Pentecost   14
Twenty-Eighth Sunday in Ordinary Time/Proper 23

Twenty-Second Sunday after Pentecost   21
Twenty-Ninth Sunday in Ordinary Time/Proper 24

Twenty-Third Sunday after Pentecost   28
Thirtieth Sunday in Ordinary Time/Proper 25

Twenty-Fourth Sunday after Pentecost   36
Thirty-First Sunday in Ordinary Time/Proper 26

Twenty-Fifth Sunday after Pentecost   43
Thirty-Second Sunday in Ordinary Time/Proper 27

Twenty-Sixth Sunday after Pentecost   50
Thirty-Third Sunday in Ordinary Time/Proper 28

Christ the King/Last Sunday after Pentecost   57
Last Sunday in Ordinary Time/Proper 29

Twentieth Sunday after Pentecost
Twenty-Seventh Sunday in Ordinary Time/Proper 22

Lectionary	First Lesson	Psalm	Second Lesson	Gospel
Revised Common	Hab. 1:1-4, 2:1-4 or Lam. 1:1-6	Ps. 37:1-9 or Lam. 3:19-26 or Ps. 137	2 Tim. 1:1-14	Luke 17:5-10
Episcopal (BCP)	Hab. 1:1-6, (7-11), 12-13; 2:1-4	Ps. 37:1-18 or 37: 3-10	2 Tim. 1:(1-5), 6-14	Luke 17:5-10
Roman Catholic	Hab. 1:2-3; 2:2-4	Ps. 95:1-2, 6-9	2 Tim. 1:6-8, 13-14	Luke 17:5-10
Lutheran (LBW)	Hab. 1:1-3; 2:1-4	Ps. 95:6-11	2 Tim. 1:3-14	Luke 17:1-10

Exegesis

FIRST LESSON: HABAKKUK 1:1-4; 2:1-4

The prophet Habakkuk, whose words are preserved in the book of his name, evidently flourished sometime in the period 608–598 B.C.E. It was a time of sudden shifts in power politics in and around the kingdom of Judah; the details are hard for us to keep straight, but it is worth making the effort. During the seventh century B.C.E. Assyria had grown weaker and slowly loosened her grip on Judah. In 612 the capital of Assyria, Nineveh (in what is today *northern* Iraq), fell to the Babylonians (the power centered in what is now *southern* Iraq). Egypt then asserted her power over Judah in an effort to keep the Babylonians at bay. It was at the instigation of Egypt that King Jehoiakim came to power in Judah in 609, and thus he paid tribute to Egypt. But then in 605 Babylonian pressure forced Jehoiakim to shift allegiance, so that he sent tribute money to Babylon instead.

The selection of verses that make up this reading distort to some degree what Habakkuk seems to have intended. Three matters need discussion. The first is the background of the two sections that make up the reading. The second is the question whether the last line of 2:4, so important to Christians in view of Paul's citation of it in Rom. 1:17, is really the content of the "vision" (2:2) and the climax of the passage. The third is what specifically is implied by "live" in 2:4.

As to the background of the two sections that make up the reading, the material in the book from 1:2 to 2:4 comprises two sequences of prophetic complaint and divine response; the first part of the reading today (1:2-4) is Habakkuk's *first* complaint, and the second part (2:1-4) makes up God's *second* response. The selection of only the first and last portions of 1:2—2:4 thus oversimplifies the message of this portion of the book.

The background of the first complaint is evidently the slack situation within Judah under King Jehoiakim: the words of judgment, "violence and destruction" (v. 3), are also found in Jer. 6:7 and would reflect the same background. Habakkuk laments that the situation in his day is one in which injustice prevails. Then in 1:5-11 God answers that he is rousing the Chaldeans (that is, the Babylonians) to punish the Judeans. Habakkuk complains a second time (1:12-17): the response of God shocks him, since the Chaldeans are more guilty than the Judeans whom they punish (v. 13). The Chaldeans treat people merely like fish to be caught (vv. 15-17).

Then comes the second portion of the reading, 2:1-4. The prophet waits to hear God's response (v. 1). God tells him to write the "vision" so that anyone may read it easily (vv. 2-3). Though readers have tended to assume that this vision is embodied in the familiar words of v. 4b, a recent commentator, J. J. M. Roberts, in *Nahum, Habakkuk, and Zephaniah: A Commentary* (Louisville: Westminster John Knox, 1991 [111, 116, 128, 148–58]) suggests rather that the vision God vouchsafes is embodied in *the whole of chapter 3*; by this understanding v. 4 simply offers two contrasting *responses* to the vision yet to be revealed.

Nevertheless the fact that Paul cites Hab. 2:4b in Rom. 1:17, and that this first reading closes with that half-verse, renders that phrase a climax for those of us who use this selection of verses in the lectionary. As we might suspect, however, the line in Habakkuk may not have carried to Habakkuk's hearers quite what Rom. 1:17 would later mean to Paul and his readers. Let us leave Romans aside, therefore, and concentrate on the meaning of the phrase in Habakkuk. We are accustomed to the rendering of the KJV, "The righteous live by their faith." But how are we to understand the original meaning of the phrase? Since the notion of resurrection, or eternal life, is alien to the Old Testament in this period, and since an individual righteous (or innocent) person certainly does *not* always survive—a matter as plain to Habakkuk as to us—then are we to understand that it is the *company* of righteous people who will survive?—or that individuals live by their faithfulness for their rest of their lives? But there is another possibility, again suggested by Roberts, and that is that the word usually translated "faith" refers not to the faith of the righteous person but to the *reliability of the vision*: he translates, "But the righteous person will live by its faithfulness." The verse thus ends on a hopeful note. But all these considerations undercut to some degree a traditional Christian understanding of the passage, making homiletical interpretation more difficult (see below).

TWENTIETH SUNDAY AFTER PENTECOST/PROPER 22

ALTERNATIVE FIRST LESSON: LAMENTATIONS 1:1-6

The five chapters of the book of Lamentations are five laments over the fall of Jerusalem in 587 B.C.E. The first four of these chapters are in the form of acrostics: successive verses begin with successive letters of the Hebrew alphabet. This form allows the poet to explore his lamentation completely—as we would say, "from A to Z."

Therefore the lesson, consisting of the first six verses of chapter 1, only begins the poet's lament. The verses before us paint a picture of the desolation of Jerusalem and the exile of its citizens. The passage offers (in contrast to the reading from Habakkuk) a picture of unrelieved gloom.

SECOND LESSON: 2 TIMOTHY 1:1-14

Timothy had been Paul's traveling companion (Acts 16:1-5). The circumstance assumed by the book of 2 Timothy is Paul's imprisonment in Rome (1:8, 16-17; 2:9; compare Acts 28:16). But it is not likely that the apostle Paul himself wrote this letter, in spite of seemingly personal notes like 4:9-16. Though the sequence 4:6-8 (part of the reading for the Twenty-Third Sunday after Pentecost) certainly does sound like Paul, one could raise the question whether the historical Paul would have praised his own success without mentioning at the same time his weakness and would have referred to his own actions without mentioning the action of God. The letter is then much more likely to have been written by a disciple of Paul a generation or two after Paul's death in order to continue the apostle's teaching in fresh circumstances, and in the present work I shall use quotation marks in referring to the writer and the recipient of the letter ("Paul"; "Timothy").

The recipient is held up as an ideal minister of the faith, the faith "Timothy" is presumed to have received from his mother and grandmother (vv. 3-7). He is enjoined to hold fast to that faith, even in the face of suffering, suffering which he would share with "Paul" (vv. 8-14).

GOSPEL: LUKE 17:5-10

Luke arranges his material so that a great number of pericopes are gathered in the context of the narrative of Jesus' journey to Jerusalem (9:51—18:14). The narrative of this journey is broken into three segments, marked by notations that he was on his way to that destination, namely 9:51; 13:22; and 17:11. The present reading is thus the completion of the second of the three segments. Verses 1-10 contain four brief teachings, which are unrelated to each other except for the references to "disciples" or "apostles."

Verses 1-2 (or 3a) offer "do not cause one of these little ones to stumble," and vv. 3 (or 3b)-4 teach the necessity for constant forgiveness.

Then in vv. 5-6, which begin the reading for today, the disciples ask Jesus to increase their faith, and Jesus offers the comparison with the mustard seed. This passage is taken from "Q," being found also in Matt. 17:20, though in Matthew it is a mountain rather than a mulberry tree that is moved.

In the context of Luke's travel narrative the request of the disciples comes on abruptly, without any preparation, again in contrast to the narrative in Matthew, where it is prepared for by the story of the healing of the epileptic boy and Jesus' subsequent statement that the disciples are of "little faith." Yet the narrative here in Luke also implies that the disciples are of little faith, since, even though the condition in Greek is a real one (literally, "if you have faith . . ."), the conclusion is of unreal form (not "you can say . . ." but "you could say . . ."). Both Matthew and Luke, then, preserve in different ways a tradition that Jesus was not impressed by the disciples' faith. First-century hearers of the passage then could be allowed to identify with the disciples' lack of faith, or even judge themselves superior to them. In any event, genuine faith can bring about quite unexpected results.

Verses 7-10 offer a narrative found only in Luke. Here Jesus teaches his disciples the appropriateness of saying, "We are worthless slaves" (other versions translate "unprofitable servants"). For us the distinction between "servant" and "slave" is crucial; a slave is owned by the master and has no freedom to leave, whereas a servant simply works for a master and can break off the relation. But neither Hebrew nor Greek made this distinction: the important thing was that such a person took orders and was not the social equal of the master.

Jesus' words presuppose a small farmer who has one worker, who not only works the farm ("plowing or tending sheep") but also prepares his meals. As to the adjective here ("worthless" or "unprofitable"), its meaning is not altogether clear. Sometimes it really means "useless" or "worthless," as in Matt. 25:30, for the servant who has done nothing. But there is no implication of that connotation here: the fellow has simply done what he was expected to do. On the other hand, there is no way that the disciples, and by extension other Christians, can claim they have done *more* than their due, or that they are worthy of God's graciousness. So a word which must often have been used as a shout to a worker for unsatisfactory work ("Unprofitable fellow!") has an appropriateness here. God's graciousness is sheer gift.

Homiletical Interpretation

All four of these passages emerge from epochs of violence and social disarray. The passage from Habakkuk, from the period before the fall of Jerusalem, reflects the situation when the Babylonians were a nightmare threat. The passage from Lamentations reflects the utter desolation of the city just after it had fallen. Jesus' teachings come from a time when crucifixions were a commonplace. Second Timothy comes from a time when one could become lost in the anonymity of the wider Mediterranean world. All four passages move hearers today to ponder questions of discipleship and faith. All four urge on us a mode of living far removed from the ordinariness of the life around us. But given the fact that the specific themes of the three readings one chooses will be at best only loosely related to one another, the preacher might be advised to select one of them for a central text and refer to the others only in passing, if at all.

The passage about the mustard seed (Luke 17:6) attracts us: the image has become a kind of cliché among many Christians.

In a community where I once served a church lived a woman named Beth. She was in her sixties at the time, overweight, bedridden from the effects of a massive stroke, waited on by her devoted husband. Word came to me that she wanted to be baptized and received into the church.

She could not use her hands. She could not speak, but she understood what was said to her, answering questions with gestures for "yes" and "no." And, surprisingly, she could still spell, so we would laboriously use a child's blackboard, where the letters and numbers were displayed, by which she might communicate. "Is the letter in this line?" A nod. "Is it A? B?" and so on, until a word or phrase emerged.

In the course of time I did baptize her, at her bedside, in the presence of a deacon or two, and accepted her into membership, and I would visit her regularly. During these visits, one request came up again and again: "PS 23"—the Twenty-Third Psalm. She wanted me to recite the Twenty-Third Psalm to her. I was glad to do it, of course, but from time to time I tried to introduce her to other psalms as well. But no, she could not be bothered with complications. As far as I could determine, her faith began and ended with the Twenty-Third Psalm (and the Lord's Prayer!). Yet who is to assess the scope of such a faith? If it was the size of a mustard seed, as I was surely tempted to assume, nevertheless we are assured that a faith of that size can remove mulberry trees (or mountains!).

On the other hand, those of us who work hard for God, who are tempted to rack up points for ourselves, hear that we are "worthless slaves." If God seems to go easy on the Beths of this world, God seems at the same time to treat unfeelingly those of us who try to do the right thing and make the world a better place. It isn't fair!

And there are further matters to consider. None of us has ever been a slaveholder, and few of us have been in a position to have absolute control over the lives and wills of others such as is implied by slaveholding. And at the same time not too many of us have been prisoners of war, or in domestic prisons for long enough to experience the lack of freedom implied by the status of slaves. It requires an extreme effort of the imagination, therefore, to conjure up an understanding of what it means to be "worthless slaves."

Furthermore (and this is a consideration that Americans in particular would do well to ponder), many of us have little experience dealing with servants. A hundred years ago, on small farms in many parts of the country, the "hired man" ate with the family, and today a young person from Europe working as an *au pair* eats with the host family. But in Jesus' saying the slave is expected to eat later; Jesus took it for granted that slaves are in an altogether different category than are masters.

Many of us are tempted to see God as a kind of senior buddy, somebody like ourselves at our best, but much more powerful. It is salutary, then, to allow Jesus' saying to cut across our urge to domesticate God, and across our passion for being appreciated by God: in short, to put ourselves into a very different mode, wherein we do our all for God, not in the expectation of any reward at all but out of sheer love and devotion to the Author of our souls.

If we choose to focus on the passage in 2 Timothy, we will find that, though not every detail of this passage fits every one of us, many details can leap out from the page. The passage glows with the affection "Paul" has for "Timothy," and with the urging that "Timothy" remember what he has gained from the faith of Lois and Eunice. (Acts 16:1 indicates that Eunice was a believer but says nothing abut Lois.)

The word *rekindle* attracts our attention. "Timothy" had been ordained ("laying on of hands"), but his (and our) awareness of the gift (Greek *charisma*) of God may flag and need rekindling. The gift casts out fear (compare Rom. 8:15).

Again, "join with me in suffering for the gospel": the writers and readers of this letter knew what it was like to be imprisoned for the faith, and the threat of martyrdom for the faith was always present. And our twentieth century has certainly seen hosts of instances of the imprisonment or martyrdom of believers. Nevertheless, these circumstances are not likely to be the fate of too many of us. On the other hand, many of us do find that the gospel leads us to be engaged in tasks we would otherwise not choose: to be faithful to our commitments when it is not easy—in our personal relationships, in our work, in public life. The trick is "not to be ashamed" (vv. 8, 12) and in general to hold our heads high.

Finally, we may find ourselves threatened by being swept away by public events past any control of ours: the passages from both Habakkuk and Lamentations testify to that. Habakkuk saw the awesome cruelty of Babylon on the horizon, and the poets who wrote the chapters of Lamentations knew it firsthand.

In 604 B.C.E. the Philistine city of Ashkelon, on the southern coast of Palestine, was destroyed by the Babylonians. In recent years the remains of the city have been excavated. One of the archaeologists records what was found. "In one of the shops of the Bazaar, . . . we found the skeleton of a middle-aged woman, about 35 years old, who had been crouching down among the storage jars, attempting to hide from the attackers. When we found her, she was lying on her back, her legs flexed and akimbo, her left arm reaching toward her head. . . . The woman had been clubbed in the head with a blunt instrument" (Lawrence E. Stager, "The Fury of Babylon: Ashkelon and the Archaeology of Destruction," *Biblical Archaeology Review* 22/1 [Jan./Feb. 1996]: 77).

There is, of course, for none of us any any guarantee that we are exempt from violence, but the affirmation of Habakkuk, particularly as restated by Paul, is that God takes care of those who are faithful, whether on this side of the grave or on the other side.

The life of faith and the marks of discipleship continually catch us off guard.

Twenty-First Sunday after Pentecost
Twenty-Eighth Sunday in Ordinary Time/Proper 23

Lectionary	First Lesson	Psalm	Second Lesson	Gospel
Revised Common	2 Kings 5:1-3, 7-15c or Jer. 29:1, 4-7	Psalm 111 or Ps. 66:1-12	2 Tim. 2:8-15	Luke 17:11-19
Episcopal (BCP)	Ruth 1:(1-7), 8-19a	Psalm 113	2 Tim. 2:(3-7), 8-15	Luke 17:11-19
Roman Catholic	2 Kings 5:14-17	Ps. 98:1-4	2 Tim. 2:8-13	Luke 17:11-19
Lutheran (LBW)	Ruth 1:1-19a	Psalm 111	2 Tim. 2:8-13	Luke 17:11-19

Exegesis

FIRST LESSON: 2 KINGS 5:1-3, 7-15c

The early chapters of 2 Kings chronicle events in Israel (the northern kingdom) and Judah (the southern kingdom) during the ninth century B.C.E. In the midst of these narratives there is inserted, in 4:1—8:6, a cycle of ten wonder-stories of the prophet Elisha, who lived in Samaria, the capital of Israel. After the stories of the jar of oil, the son restored to life, the spoiled pot of stew, and the twenty loaves, comes the fifth story, that of the healing and conversion of Naaman the Syrian, which takes up the whole of chapter 5. The verses selected for this lesson therefore present only a portion of that story.

Verses 1-3 give the background. Naaman was a general serving the king of Aram (the Syrians). At that time the Aramean kingdom was a third power in the area alongside Israel and Judah; one has the impression that the Arameans held the upper hand at the moment. Naaman suffered from some kind of skin disease ("leprosy" in the text). An Israelite girl, having been captured in a raid, had become a slave to Naaman's wife, and the girl, concerned for Naaman, expressed the wish that Elisha ("the prophet who is in Samaria") might have the opportunity to cure him.

The omitted verses tell how Naaman passed this notion on to his king, whereupon the king sent Naaman to the king of Israel with a letter of introduction and an enormous gift. The letter simply expressed the wish that the Israelite king cure Naaman, but without any mention of Elisha, who was after all, from the point of view of the palace, a marginal figure. (These details are crucial enough to the story that, if this reading is chosen, the intervening verses might well be included.)

The king of Israel of course had no particular skills in curing skin diseases, and in despair he tore his clothes, since he could only conclude that the Aramean king was trying to pick a quarrel with him. Elisha, on learning of the king's distress, sent him a letter telling him to send Naaman on, "that he may learn that there is a prophet in Israel" (v. 8). It is clear that behind the vivid details of the story are assumptions about status and etiquette, honor and shame!

Naaman comes to Elisha's house, and since he is a general, he comes with his horses and chariots and does not deign to enter the household of a modest prophet. Elisha, for his part, does not go out to meet him but sends out a servant instead, who simply passes on the prescription: to be cured, go wash in the Jordan river seven times. But of course Naaman expected personal treatment—he expected the prophet to come out to him, to call upon the name of Yahweh, to wave his hand over the diseased area. And as for the prescription, the river Jordan is, after all, really a very modest watercourse alongside the great rivers that flow through Damascus; this rustic has made a fool of him! His servants had to calm his rage with wiser words: He would certainly have done a hard thing gladly—why not try something easy?

And, according to the story, he really was cured, and he returned to Elisha humbled and willing to proclaim the sole reality and effectiveness of the God of Israel.

The remainder of the narrative goes on to deal with other striking details. Elisha refused to take payment. Naaman, now a believer in Yahweh, hauls a wheelbarrow-load of Israelite earth back to Syria with him so that he can stand on soil appropriate for the worship of the true God. And finally we hear of the greed manifested by Elisha's servant Gehazi for some of the proferred payment that Elisha had refused. Though beyond the verses chosen for the reading, these matters, too, entice one with preaching opportunities.

ALTERNATIVE FIRST LESSON: JEREMIAH 29:1, 4-7

Jeremiah 29 contains the text of a letter the prophet sent from Jerusalem to Jews in Babylon. It should be remembered that Jerusalem fell twice to the Babylonians: the first time was in 598 B.C.E., after which Nebuchadnezzar took away many Jews to exile and placed Zedekiah on the throne. The second time was eleven years later, in 587, when the city walls, the temple, and the palace were destroyed and once more many leading citizens, including Zedekiah, were exiled to Babylon. Jeremiah's letter was written from Jerusalem to the first group of exiles, probably in 594, when there was agitation in the Babylonian court to overthrow Nebuchadnezzar. (Some of the background can be found in 2 Kings 24:10-17.)

Verse 1 introduces the matter and vv. 4-7 contain a crucial portion of Jeremiah's message, which is a word from God (v. 4): the exiles are not to consider themselves prisoners, enduring empty days while waiting for release. Instead they are to put down roots, build houses, plant gardens, and establish families.

Verse 7 is the surprising climax of the portion chosen for the reading, playing on the implications of the Hebrew word *shalom*. We must understand that ancient letters began with a notice of the name of the sender and the name of the addressee, followed by an expression with *shalom* ("peace"), such as "A, to B: Peace to you and your household." The beginning of Paul's letter to the Romans is a good (and elaborate) example of the form: "Paul" (v. 1), "to all God's beloved in Rome" (v. 7a); "grace to you and peace" (v. 7b). But though Jer. 29:4 names the sender ("the Lord of hosts") and the addressees ("to all the exiles . . ."), it offers no greeting of "peace." Instead it plunges (rather rudely, therefore) directly into the body of the message ("build houses . . ."). The recipients are waiting for the word of *shalom*; they get it only in v. 7, where in the NRSV it is translated "welfare." The implication is, if you seek *shalom*, then first "seek the *shalom* of the city where I have sent you into exile, and pray to the Lord on its behalf, for in its *shalom* you will find your *shalom*." Jeremiah passes on to his fellow Jews the word he has had from God: pray for your oppressors and their *shalom*; only then will you merit the *shalom* you have expected in the courtesies of correspondence.

SECOND LESSON: 2 TIMOTHY 2:8-15

The span of this reading breaks what seem to be the shape of the letter: v. 8 of chapter 2 does seem to begin a new section, but v. 15 hardly closes a section, coming in the midst of instruction to the pastor (vv. 14-19). Verses 8-10 offer "Paul's" urging of the gospel on "Timothy," a gospel which "Paul" proclaims even in the midst of the sufferings of prison. Verses 11-13 are in the style of a hymn and are perhaps to be understood as the citation of a liturgy of baptism. Verses 14-15 are "Paul's" urging on "Timothy" not to get involved with profitless argumentation but to stick to the "word of truth."

GOSPEL: LUKE 17:11-19

Here begins the third of the three sections of the journey to Jerusalem in Luke. This lesson is the narrative of the cleansing of ten lepers, though one might well call it "the story of the grateful Samaritan." This healing narrative is found only in Luke. Since both vv. 11 and 19 contain several of Luke's favorite expressions, one could imagine that these opening and closing verses represent Luke's own editing of material that came from a pre-Lukan source. But as for vv. 11 and 19, if v. 19 is a fine Lukan climax, v. 11 is an evidence of utter geographical confusion—since Samaria and Galilee really border each other, what indeed is meant by "the region between Samaria and Galilee"? One must conclude that Luke writes as someone from outside Palestine; fortunately the geographical details are not crucial to the narrative.

It is clear that the story is modeled to some degree on the story of the healing of Naaman (in the wording of the Greek Septuagint, of course). Though it is a healing story, the emphasis turns from the healing to the distinctive gratitude of the one Samaritan who was healed (vv. 15-18).

Homiletical Interpretation

The two alternative Old Testament lessons and the Gospel lesson are united by the theme of the extension of God's grace beyond the narrowly construed boundaries of the covenant people: in the passage from 2 Kings it was the Syrian general Naaman whom God healed through the prophet Elisha; in the passage from Jeremiah it was prayers for the Babylonians that God enjoined on the Jews; and in the Gospel it was ten lepers, among whom was a grateful Samaritan, whom Jesus healed. One reason to choose the Naaman narrative is of course the fact that both the Naaman story and the Gospel lesson are healing stories (and, as pointed out in the exegesis, the shape of the Gospel story is modeled on that of the healing of Naaman). The reading from 2 Timothy does not share the theme of the extension of God's grace beyond the conventional boundaries of the covenant people, though perhaps one could stretch the expression "The word of God is not chained" (v. 9) to include it.

If one chooses to expound on the two healing stories, then one needs to ponder the matter of sickness and healing in the Bible. It is almost impossible for present-day hearers in the United States to grasp the situation of men and women and children who lack the sort of medical help we take for granted today. Several decades ago I was on the staff one summer of the archaeological excavation at Shechem on the West Bank in Palestine. More than once a Palestinian worker would come to me and ask me for an aspirin. I would fetch him one from the first-aid box kept at the dig headquarters, but as I did so I would ponder the sort of life lived by people for whom even aspirin tablets are not normally available. Thus, unless we have served overseas as Peace Corps workers or in some other way lived among ordinary folk in the Third World, we are not likely to know what it is like to live with undiagnosed illness, with unrelievable pain, and with the despair that accompanies them. How many of the psalms in the Psalter reflect the laments of folk who are ill!—Psalm 88 is a noteworthy example.

Skin ailments must have been endemic in communities where people lived close together, did not bathe regularly, and were subject to the bites of fleas and other pests. And of course these folk were not diagnosticians. Though translations of the Bible continue to use the term *leprosy*, it is clear that the Hebrew term covered any number of afflictions of the skin: the fact that the same word translated "leprosy" could be used for conditions on the walls of houses (Lev. 14:34-53)—evidently in reference to mold on building stones or plaster—suggests that the term did not necessarily refer to the leprosy we now call "Hansen's disease." And we should remind ourselves, as we think about skin ailments, that they often have a strong psychological component, as any present-day dermatologist can confirm.

With these observations let us turn to the biblical narratives. God is understood to be the author of both sickness and healing, so that men of God, prophets and the like, could be expected to effect cures. Elijah, it was said, raised to life again the son of the widow at Zarephath (1 Kings 17:17-24), and Elisha in similar fashion was remembered as raising the son of the Shunammite woman (2 Kings 4:8-37). There is no way, of course, to assess the historical reliability of these tales from the books of Kings: they evidently stem from the traditions of villagers whose monotonous lives would occasionally be punctuated by events of wonder. Of course, there might well have been many men and women in biblical times who claimed to speak and act for God but who did *not* perform such wonders, or who tried to and failed, but of course no stories would survive of these nonevents. It was the stunning stories of healings achieved that would testify to the power of God and would be remembered and passed on to later generations and eventually be gathered into the biblical tradition of the mighty acts of God.

By the testimony of the narrative, then, Naaman was desperate enough to seek help from a prophet who was living in what was for him foreign territory, much as an Englishman living in India in the 1920s might seek a cure for his seemingly incurable disease from a local Hindu holy man. (Who knows what powers there might be beyond the knowledge of rational Europe?—nothing is lost by trying!) Naaman of course had his own ideas about how a proper cure would be effected, and it was a blow to his pride to be subjected to the seemingly casual and offhand treatment proffered him by Elisha. But Naaman did gain the cure he sought after all, and of course the Israelites for their part gained a story of the wonder effected by the local man of God, by the local river, and by the God they proclaimed to be the author of sickness and health.

And it is clear that Jesus, for his part, was a healer. We can say this not just out of the faith we may have in the reliability of the Gospel accounts, but also out of the intensive scrutiny that modern scholars have given to those Gospel accounts. To be sure, there have been many folk who have been impatient with the miraculous narratives in the Gospels and have sought to delete the healings and other miracles from their understanding of Jesus; Thomas Jefferson was one of those who have made such an effort. But the healings are so inextricably woven into the narratives of Jesus that to take them out is to be left with little of the Jesus of history.

There is no reason, then, to dismiss this story of the healing of the ten lepers as simply the product of the excessive piety of first-century Christians—it is a narrative we can hear without hesitation. As we watch the scene we might wish to ponder the desolation of these men called "lepers," living outside the reassurance that normal community life can offer, and their eagerness for any turn from their hopeless situation. The reputation of Jesus must have preceded him on the road, and the positive expectations of these "lepers" must have played a part in their healing. But of course thoughts like these were far from the mindset of the first-century Christians who passed on the story: for them it is one more marvelous testimony to the power of Jesus to take folk out of the realm of shame, of pain, of hopelessness—the realm of Satan, that is, and to restore them to the realm of God—the realm of joy, of wholeness, of confidence.

But, as we have noticed, the story is more than an account of healing; it is a story of ingratitude and gratitude. Can we believe that nine out of ten people who have their health restored forget to say "thank you"? Is this proportion intended to be typical, or is the proportion exaggerated in order to highlight the response of the one leper who is a Samaritan? Exaggerated or not, clearly Jesus never had the impulse to be idealistic about the goodness of human nature; and those of us with experience with a cross section of human beings may be inclined, in our darker moments, to affirm that nine out of ten is about right.

There is the one grateful fellow, however, and he is a Samaritan! Luke has prepared us with an illustration of the normal attitude of Samaritans to Jews (9:51-56) and the striking parable of the compassion of the Good Samaritan (10:29-37), so one hardly needs to be reminded of the status of Samaritans in first-century Palestine. These folk were the heirs of the religious tradition preserved in the north; their sanctuary was located at the northern city of Shechem (compare John 4:9, 20). Clearly enmity can be great between communities of people who argue about different interpretations of a common heritage, and so it was with Jews and Samaritans. In the narrative the Samaritan is a "foreigner" (v. 18). The healing of this man, then, is a noteworthy example of Jesus' touch beyond his Jewish community, and thus matches the healing of Naaman the Syrian in the first reading.

A further word must be said about the alternative reading in which Jeremiah enjoins the exiles in Babylon to pray for their oppressors. Few things are harder. Secretaries who must work under bosses who are petty, arbitrary, and vindictive know this. Army trainees who suffer under brutish first sergeants know this. The raucous talk in barracks after hours, or the snickers around the water cooler, will be proof of this. In such circumstances people usually keep their morale up with jokes, stories, and pranks. Slaves in the American South told Bre'r Rabbit stories. To pray for one's oppressors, then, may be a spiritual gain, but the psychic cost is great, and the wonder is that an Old Testament prophet could pass on such instructions from God.

And a final word must be said about the passage from 2 Timothy. Almost any of the phrases in this reading offer themselves for preaching, but perhaps the one that leaps out most strikingly from the page is "The word of God is not chained" (v. 9). The Bible from beginning to end affirms the power of God's word, the creating word, the effective word, the transforming word; and the history of both synagogue and church proclaims the same. Christians particularly, who know God's word to be incarnate in Jesus Christ (John 1:1-18), know that word, proclaim it, live it, and celebrate it.

Twenty-Second Sunday after Pentecost
Twenty-Ninth Sunday in Ordinary Time/Proper 24

Lectionary	First Lesson	Psalm	Second Lesson	Gospel
Revised Common	Gen. 32:22-31 or Jer. 31:27-34	Psalm 121 or Ps. 119:97-104	2 Tim. 3:14—4:5	Luke 18:1-8
Episcopal (BCP)	Gen. 32:3-8, 22-30	Psalm 121	2 Tim. 3:14—4:5	Luke 18:1-8a
Roman Catholic	Exod. 17:8-13	Ps. 121:1-8	2 Tim. 3:14—4:2	Luke 18:1-8
Lutheran (LBW)	Gen. 32:22-30	Psalm 121	2 Tim. 3:14—4:5	Luke 18:1-8a

Exegesis

FIRST LESSON: GENESIS 32:22-31

This is the climactic event in the story of Jacob. We recall the outline of the story. Jacob had obtained Esau's birthright in exchange for a pot of lentil stew, and then by trickery he had obtained the blessing from Isaac that was rightfully Esau's. He set out quickly to go east to his mother's homeland, not only to seek a wife but to be out of the way of Esau as well. He was taken into the household of Laban, his mother's brother. He asked for Laban's daughter Rachel for a wife, worked for seven years to obtain her, only to receive her older sister Leah instead, and then worked another seven years to gain Rachel. From these wives and their handmaids eleven sons were born, and Jacob prospered in livestock as well. Laban became steadily more jealous of Jacob, so that the latter finally fled from Laban's household without any farewells, taking with him his wives, his children and his flocks. Now Jacob had incurred the enmity not only of Esau but of Laban.

When Laban learned of Jacob's flight, he pursued his son-in-law and overtook him. After uneasy negotiations, they managed to make a covenant with each other (31:43-54). Jacob then turned his attention to the inevitable encounter with his brother Esau. When he learned that Esau was approaching with a retinue of four hundred men, he prayed a panic-stricken prayer to God that he and his family might be delivered from his brother. He arranged to send enormous gifts ahead to Esau, really bribes.

And now the verses of the lesson! For reasons that are not clear, Jacob sent his wives, their two maids, his eleven sons, and his other belongings, presumably including his livestock, ahead across the stream of the Jabbok river, while he himself stayed behind for the night; were there still belongings left behind that needed to be guarded? And now suddenly the vivid details of the narrative become mysterious indeed: he became engaged in a wrestling match with a man until daybreak. His antagonist was a stranger who is understood to represent God, and in the morning, not having been bested by his opponent, he received a new name, Israel. Then in the ensuing narrative Jacob was able to effect a reconciliation with Esau, though, as with his meeting with Laban, it was not without mutual suspicion.

Much in the narrative of the wrestling match remains confusing to the hearer: doubtless it was a story that was shaped and reshaped through many centuries, taking on fresh understandings as it was retold. As it stands, it sounds for one thing like a narrative to explain the name given to the city of Penuel (or Peniel—vv. 30-31). But what do those references to the "hip socket" mean (vv. 31, 32)? Above all, how are we really to understand the whole experience of the wrestling match? Was it a vivid dream? Is the "man" (vv. 24, 25, 28) to be understood as an angel, as the later text in Hos. 12:4 maintains? Whatever the meaning of the details, it is clear that the narrative is a foundation story for the people of the Old Testament: it is the moment when Jacob, and therefore his descendants, receive the new name "Israel."

The name is interpreted (v. 28) as meaning "the one who strives with God," but the text goes on to say, "for you have striven with God *and with humans*, and have prevailed." True, Jacob has striven with God, if his wrestling opponent represents God, but who are the humans?—Laban and Esau, presumably, but then his meeting with Esau is still to come. To add to our puzzlement, the etymology of the name "Israel" cannot really be "one who strives with God," but rather "God strives" (see the footnote in the NRSV). So what we have here may be the traditional designation for the covenant people that has been reinterpreted in the light of the story of the wrestling match. In any event, a new name suggests a new identity (compare the change of Abram's name to Abraham; Gen. 17:5), so Jacob's new name betokens his destiny as the father of the covenant people.

ALTERNATIVE FIRST LESSON: JEREMIAH 31:27-34

This passage consists of three short sequences, vv. 27-28, 29-30, and 31-34; all of them are statements about events to take place in time to come. Verses 27-28 embody a general statement: the covenant people will be subject not to destruction but to rebuilding. Then in vv. 29-30 it is said that people will no longer repeat a traditional proverb, "The parents have eaten sour grapes, and the children's teeth are set on edge." The proverb refers in picturesque fashion to the traditional solidarity between the generations in matters of responsibility for conduct (compare Exod. 34:7b). No: in time to come each person shall be responsible simply for his or her own wrongdoing, not for the wrongdoing of parents or children. Both vv. 27-28 and 29-30 give evidence of being added secondarily by later editors to the collection of genuine oracles of the prophet Jeremiah. In particular, vv. 29-30 appear to be a summary of Ezek. 18:1-4: that chapter of Ezekiel embodies the prophet's perception that the traditional notion of corporate personality—the idea that members of families are tied together in their identities and their responsibilities—must give way to an understanding of individual responsibility. But the adaptation of Ezekiel's word here in Jeremiah appears to be an effort, after Jeremiah's time, to mitigate the radicalism of the "new covenant" passage in vv. 31-34.

The new covenant passage, however, does appear to be authentic to the prophet Jeremiah: it has all the marks of his diction. One could imagine it being proclaimed in the autumn of the year 587 B.C.E. We recall that in the summer of that year Jerusalem had fallen to the Babylonians for the second and final time; the Babylonian general had burned the public buildings of the city and demolished its defense wall (39:1-8). Yet in the autumn came the occasion of the festival of booths and the day of atonement; it may have been the year to read the law of Deuteronomy once more (see Deut. 31:9-13). If so, Jeremiah could have offered this pronouncement as a counter-proclamation to the reading of Deuteronomy, with its emphasis on covenant (see Deut. 4:23 and often).

And what a radical pronouncement it is! The Israelites had always assumed that the covenant that God had made with them was forever (compare Gen. 17:7). Here, by contrast, is the word that that covenant is *at an end*, inasmuch as the Israelites had broken it past mending (v. 32). But God, ever innovative, is drawing up a new covenant that they will be unable to break. Instead of a law written on stone, as the Ten Commandments were, a law which they regularly broke, the law in the new covenant will be written on their hearts (v. 33)—actually "heart" (singular), as if in time to come the covenant community will have but a single heart and mind. Instead of the necessity of mutual reminders of the obligation to God, the covenant community will have a knowledge of God by definition, so that iniquity and sin will be a thing of the past (v. 34).

If the narrative of Jacob's wrestling with the stranger at the Jabbok (see above) was a foundation story for the Old Testament people, this passage from Jeremiah is foundational for the New Testament people. In the narratives of the Last Supper Jesus is remembered as saying, "This cup is the new covenant in my blood" (1 Cor. 11:25). Paul, in 2 Cor. 3:7-18, contrasts the old covenant with the Spirit of Christ now present in the church. And the whole passage in Jeremiah is cited in full in Heb. 8:8-12 (and vv. 33-34 are cited once more, in part, in Heb. 10:16-17). Indeed, the very word *testament* means "covenant"; through the "new testament" Christians understand themselves to be covenanted with God in the way set forth in this passage in Jeremiah.

SECOND LESSON: 2 TIMOTHY 3:14—4:5

This sequence is plucked out of the closing exhortations of the epistle, exhortations that appear to start in 3:10 and continue through 4:8. The first verses of the reading reflect the same kind of advice as in the second reading two weeks ago: stay firm in the faith of your childhood (compare 1:5-6). Proclaim the message; endure suffering (compare 1:8).

One verse here has caught the attention of many Christians, v. 16. This is usually understood as "All scripture is inspired by God" (so the RSV), but two matters need attention. The first is that, for the author, "scripture" did not of course include the New Testament—it was the Old Testament (and, one might note, not in the original Hebrew but in the Greek Septuagint translation). The New Testament, understood as a complete body of scriptural books, was not yet in existence. The second is that the Greek expression translated "inspired by God" could well be attributive rather than the predicate—the *Revised English Bible* has so translated it: "All inspired scripture has its use for teaching the truth" (compare the NRSV margin). This translation would not necessarily imply that some scripture *lacks* inspiration, but the emphasis in the verse is clearly on the *usefulness* of scripture rather than its *inspiration*. In any event one would do well not to press a particular understanding of the verse too strongly.

GOSPEL: LUKE 18:1-8

In the course of the church year the lectionary skips over some passages in the Gospel, and so today we move past Luke 17:20-37 to today's lesson, 18:1-8, the parable of the widow and the unjust judge, another unit found only in Luke.

Verse 1 is clearly an editorial introduction to the parable; the parable proper begins with v. 2. But commentators differ where the parable ends, whether with v. 5 or v. 6; it is likely, however, that v. 6, the exclamation, is an integral part of the original parable, since the behavior of the judge is so outrageous. Verses 7-8a are then a secondary interpretation, making explicit that the judge represents God, and isolating the detail of "granting justice" (vv. 3, 5). Then v. 8b is a further elaboration, introducing the theme of the coming of the Son of Man.

The parable offers two contrasting characters—the judge, who held full power in the community, and the widow, who held no power at all, lacking a husband who might seek public vindication on behalf of the family. But she, though powerless, refuses to give up, and he, though holding the power, finally gives in to her simply because of her persistence. If the hardhearted judge gives up, how much more will God respond to our prayer! Even if God appears to be unresponsive, one must not lose heart but continue to pray for vindication. Verses 7-8 evidently relate the parable to the delay in Christ's second coming, an urgent issue in Luke's day. Though the question, "Will he delay long in helping them?" (v. 7), seems to refer to God, the closing question in v. 8 suggests that the "delay" is the final judgment, when Christ will come again.

Christians then are to pray without ceasing for final justice.

Homiletical Interpretation

These lessons, like those two weeks ago, appear to have little in common. As to the second lesson, we have already noted that the advice given to "Timothy" in the reading reflects the general field of ideas already set forth in the reading two weeks ago. The verse that will catch the eye in the reading may well be 3:16, already discussed in the exegesis: it opens the way to set forth the centrality of scripture (notably even Old Testament scripture, the scripture to which the passage has reference!) in the life of the church.

Both the Genesis lesson and the lesson from Jeremiah are foundational, and either of them would merit being the central text for preaching. Jacob the trickster became Israel, the covenant people of the Old Testament. Here is perfect evidence that the Bible does not give us example stories, since Jacob is certainly not to be a model for our conduct. The church is the "Israel of God" (Gal. 6:16); we are not to emulate Jacob but instead to marvel that God chooses unlikely folk for the working out of the divine purpose among human beings. This thought may give us hope when we are tempted to see ourselves as unfit for God's purposes.

And for many folk a life with God is an occasion for wrestling, as it was for Jacob. Christian literature is filled with testimony that one can struggle for years with God as to whose will is to prevail—Augustine's prayer, "Lord, give me chastity and continence, but not yet," comes to mind. But the experience of struggle is not a note that is often heard in genteel presentations of the faith. Jacob's wrestling match, then, and his subsequent limping, reminds us that our struggling with God may leave us crippled as well as triumphant with a new identity.

The Jeremiah text most wonderfully unites Old Testament and New Testament; we Christians have taken the prophecy for our own. But we must be careful, when we understand ourselves to be God's covenant people, that we do not wrongly assume that God has rejected the Jews. The eleventh chapter of the Letter to the Romans is clear on this matter: Gentile Christians are simply grafted onto the olive tree of Israel. The new covenant does not annul the old.

Now what was wrong with the old covenant, in Jeremiah's mind? It was an external law, written on tablets of stone. Members of the covenant people could therefore disobey it, and did. Or worse, they could obey it insincerely—with their fingers crossed behind their backs, so to speak. In the new covenant, by contrast, God's law would be written on the heart. But if in the new covenant one will obey God automatically, then, one might well ask, what becomes of human freedom? The question did not arise for Jeremiah; he simply affirmed that God's people will obey, not because they are supposed to, but because they want to.

The vision, then, is of a people so overjoyed with God's grace that obedience becomes a glad privilege rather than a dutiful obligation. And one has the impression that the earliest Christians did fulfill that vision. "Day by day, as they spent much time together in the temple, they broke bread at home and ate their food with glad and generous hearts, praising God and having the goodwill of all the people. And day by day the Lord added to their number those who were being saved" (Acts 2:46-47).

But the last verse of the passage implies that, in the new covenant, religious education committees will be a thing of the past, so Jeremiah's vision has not yet fully come to pass for most of us. But the vision is worth pursuing. What would it take for our communities of faith to be so transformed by joy and gratitude that both children and adults pick up the faith by contagion?

There may be a way to combine the readings from Genesis and Luke. For neither Jacob nor the widow were things going smoothly: Jacob prayed for rescue from Esau, and the widow begged the judge for justice against her opponent. And if the stranger at the Jabbok represents God, and if the unjust judge represents God, then in both passages the protagonist (Jacob and the widow) struggled to prevail over God. But there is of course this difference between Jacob and the widow: the widow is presumed to be deserving of justice, while Jacob had a guilty conscience about his earlier cheating of Esau, or at least he should have. But both passages do offer illustrations for effective prayer.

And so we turn to the passage in Luke once more. One detail in the parable is not often commented on, and that is the hardheartedness of the judge: he "neither feared God nor had respect for people" (v. 2), as he himself affirms (v. 4). The thought then strikes us: if the judge represents God, then what does this say about Jesus' own view of God? It is useful to recognize that the Bible does not necessarily reflect our own notions of a constantly benevolent God. Abraham needed to chide God on matters of justice (Gen. 18:25), and Job preceived God to be altogether unjust (see, for example, Job 9:12, 22). True, Jesus revealed the utter graciousness of God (see, for example, Matt. 5:45), but he offered parables that suggest that God is at least more arbitrary than we are comfortable with (compare the parable of the laborers in the vineyard in Matt. 20:1-15). Perhaps Jesus is here suggesting that even though, at least to us in the short run, God *appears* to be hardhearted and unjust, we are not to give up.

The widow certainly did not give up—she pestered the judge until she got what she was asking for. Many years ago a student posed a problem to one of his professors in a course on the developing of spiritual disciplines: "I have been praying for a particular person for a month, and nothing has happened yet." "I know," replied the professor. "I have been praying for someone everyday for twenty years, and nothing has happened yet." The need is "to pray always and not to lose heart" (v. 1).

Twenty-Third Sunday after Pentecost
Thirtieth Sunday in Ordinary Time/Proper 25

Lectionary	First Lesson	Psalm	Second Lesson	Gospel
Revised Common	Sir. 35:12-17 or Jer. 14:7-10, 19-22 or Joel 2:23-32	Ps. 84:1-7 or Psalm 65	2 Tim. 4:6-8, 16-18	Luke 18:9-14
Episcopal (BCP)	Jer. 14:(1-6), 7-10, 19-22	Psalm 84 or 84:1-6	2 Tim. 4:6-8, 16-18	Luke 18:9-14
Roman Catholic	Sir. 35:12-14, 16-17	Ps. 34:2-3, 7, 17-19, 23	2 Tim. 4:6-8, 16-18	Luke 18:9-14
Lutheran (LBW)	Deut. 10:12-22	Psalm 34	2 Tim. 4:6-8, 16-18	Luke 18:9-14

Exegesis

FIRST LESSON: SIRACH 35:12-17

Many Protestants will not have the book of Sirach (also called "the Wisdom of Ben Sira," or "Ecclesiasticus") in their Old Testaments, since it is reckoned in the Protestant Apocrypha. The book resembles Proverbs in many respects; it was written late in the Old Testament period (roughly 200–180 B.C.E.). The reading today comes on the heels of the author's advice to be generous in bringing sacrifices and tithes to the temple (vv. 10-11). Verses 12-15 continue in the same line, enjoining generosity and unselfish motives in the offering of gifts to God. Verse 15 ends with the affirmation, "with [God] there is no partiality," and then v. 16 veers off in a different direction with the same word, "He will not show partiality to the poor," and the balance of vv. 16-17 affirm that God will indeed hear the cry of the wronged, the orphan, and the widow, those folk who have no one to defend them in court.

ALTERNATIVE FIRST LESSON: JEREMIAH 14:7-10, 19-22

These verses are part of a long sequence pertaining to the emergency of a drought which the land was suffering (14:1). Given Jeremiah's description of the drought in vv. 2-6, it must have been catastrophically severe: the people responded by fasting, to try to move God to relent (v. 12). It is likely that the fasting was prescribed officially; it is tempting to associate that fasting with the fast proclaimed by "all the people in Jerusalem and all the people who came from the towns of Judah to Jerusalem" mentioned in 36:9. There would then have been an official liturgy at the Temple to pray for an end to the drought. If that was the case, then 14:1—15:9 appears to be Jeremiah's own version of a liturgy that would be *really* appropriate to the occasion.

The selected verses offer two laments voiced by the people (vv. 7-9, 19-22) enclosing a single verse of God's judgment on the people (v. 10). In both laments the people admit their iniquities (vv. 7, 20), but in spite of this wrongdoing the people cannot understand why they should be suffering (v. 19). They are desperate for God's rescue (vv. 7, 21). There is a nice pun in the word *hope* at the beginning of v. 8, inasmuch as the Hebrew *miqweh* ("hope") can also mean "pool." The cisterns are empty (v. 3), so God is not only the hope of Israel but its source of water. Jeremiah's irony is biting in his notion that the people are comparing God to a confused traveler who cannot find lodging for the night (vv. 8-9).

Jeremiah relays God's response, and it is noteworthy that not only are the people spoken of in the third person but God is as well. Jeremiah keeps both at arm's length, and one has the impression that God and the people are no longer conversation partners. "They have loved to wander" (v. 10). The last part of v. 10, beginning, "Therefore the Lord does not accept them," is a direct quotation from Hos. 8:13; the implication then is that that prophetic word from a hundred years before is now coming to pass in the drought. Given this judgment, the words of vv. 19-22 suggest that the people simply cannot hear God.

ALTERNATIVE FIRST LESSON: JOEL 2:23-32

The book of Joel is a late prophetic book, dating probably to the period 400–350 B.C.E. The immediate occasion is a terrible plague of locusts (1:2—2:11) which was understood as a prelude to the day of the Lord (1:15); it elicited a call to the people to repent (2:12-17). Then from 2:18 to the end of the book we hear words of restoration from God; the verses in the lesson are thus part of this hopeful section.

Verses 23-27 divide into two sections, vv. 23-24 and vv. 25-27; the first of these addresses the children of Zion, describing the fertility of the land in ensuing years as a motivation for praising God, who is referred to in the third person. In the second section there is a shift of diction—God speaks in the first person, continuing the description of the coming fertility of the land to replace the losses the people experienced in the locust plague (v. 25). People will have enough to eat (v. 26).

The last portion of the reading, vv. 28-32, is familiar to us because Peter cited it in his Pentecost sermon (Acts 2:17-21). It is a description of the last days. Verses 28-29 affirm that God's spirit will be poured out. "Spirit" is a vital power, a will leading to action. It is not at human disposal (the Hebrew word also means "wind"!) but is freely given by God. And it is to be poured out on everyone, male and female, old and young, master and slave; indeed on "all flesh" (v. 28). Though that expression can imply "all humanity," and although Peter at Pentecost understood it to refer to all nations, the term in Joel surely refers simply to "everybody" *in Israel* (compare the thought at the beginning of v. 27). Verses 30-32 offer other signs of the end time, portents in the heavens and on the earth (vv. 30-31); those who worship the Lord, however, are assured that they need not fear, for they will be saved (v. 32).

SECOND LESSON: 2 TIMOTHY 4:6-8, 16-18

This is the last of the readings from 2 Timothy in the lectionary. Verses 6-8 offer "Paul's" circumstances before his anticipated death. Many of the phrases in this sequence can be paralleled in passages authentic to Paul. Thus, in v. 6, compare "I am poured out as a libation" with the same expression in Phil. 2:17, and for "my departure" compare "my desire is to depart" in Phil. 1:23; in v. 7 the phrase "finish the race" reminds the hearer of the comparison in 1 Cor. 9:24-27 to running a race in a stadium. The term "his appearing" (v. 8) is evidently an expression for Christ's second coming, given the phrasing of v. 1.

Verses 16-18 offer details that appear to refer to an earlier trial that Paul underwent (compare Acts 23:1-11, the narrative of Paul's trial before the council in Jerusalem) or else to an earlier hearing in his present trial (at least as the author depicts it: compare the remarks on 2 Timothy in the exegesis for the Twentieth Sunday after Pentecost). "The lion's mouth" (v. 17) is probably to be taken metaphorically rather than be understood as a reference to real lions in the amphitheater; the author may have in mind Ps. 22:21, "Save me from the mouth of the lion"—since the references to animals in that psalm are likely to be metaphorical.

GOSPEL: LUKE 18:9-14

The parable of the Pharisee and the tax collector, like the parable of the widow and the unjust judge that precedes it, is found only in Luke. The last half of v. 14 virtually repeats 14:11, and most scholars take that sentence as having been added secondarily to the parable.

This parable, unlike that of the widow and the judge, does not have a metaphorical reach (we recall that in that parable the judge represented God); instead, like three other parables in Luke (those of the Good Samaritan, 10:29-37; the rich fool, 12:16-21; and the rich man and Lazarus, 16:19-31), it is an *example story*, a practical model for conduct.

The Pharisees figure in all four Gospels as opponents of Jesus, with the result that this group has had among Christians an utterly negative reputation—it is passages like this one that have led to the use of the adjective "pharisaical" as a description of hypocritical self-righteousness. But one needs to understand who the Pharisees were in the Jewish life of Jesus' day. They were an educated group, largely laymen, whose leadership was to be found in the smaller towns as well as in the cities. They were concerned to hold to a careful observance of Torah, developing fresh approaches of oral interpretation in the changing circumstances of the Hellenization of Palestine and Roman occupation. In a way, then, they were the "liberals" of the day, seeking to keep up with fresh questions that arose in observing the law. Jesus grew up in this atmosphere, and his differences with them were keen precisely because both he and they made it their prime concern to follow the will of God: their very differences loomed all the larger.

By contrast, tax collectors were collaborators with the Roman authorities and were therefore considered traitors to Judaism. Furthermore, they made their profit on the excess beyond what they were required to collect, so that they were seen as extortioners as well. One notes that Matthew remembers Jesus' linking tax collectors with prostitutes (Matt. 21:31-32); proper Jews did not associate with either sort.

It is worth noting that the Gospels do depict some Pharisees sympathetically (see Luke 13:31 or John 3:1), so Jesus' depiction in this parable of the boasting of the Pharisee is doubtless a parody; but those who heard the parable must have loved the details. By the same token not many tax collectors might have been so conscience-stricken as the one Jesus describes here, but there must have been at least some, like Zaccheus (19:1-10: see the Gospel for next Sunday). Jesus makes his point, then, by the contrast between the appalling boasting of the socially approved "good" man and the self-berating of the socially rejected "bad" man.

Homiletical Interpretation

It would not be easy to find a common thread among all the readings, whether one chooses Sirach, Jeremiah, or Joel for the first lesson, unless it were a general topic like God's support to those who are faithful.

The readings from Jeremiah and Luke could well be used back-to-back in a treatment of repentance. The topic of sin is one that some congregations have heard about so steadily that they may need a nuanced approach if they are to listen to the notion at all; on the other hand, there are in our own time congregations that rarely ponder the matter of sin, so that it became necessary a generation ago for Karl Menninger to write a book with the title *Whatever Became of Sin?* There was a deacon once in a congregation in which I was a member who would recite along with the congregation any confession of sin that used "we," but remain silent when the confession used "I." *His* own conscience was always clear. This may be an occasion, then, to reintroduce the matter through both Jeremiah and Luke. On the other hand, each passage could stand so splendidly on its own that either might merit the full attention of a sermon.

Let us ponder each separately, and then ponder possibilities of using both together. Jeremiah 14:7-9 is really a very funny depiction of the thoughts of people untouched by real contrition. "True," they say, "our inquities tell against us; it does look bad. But you, O God, are our hope"—and "our pool" (see the exegesis above). These people are like spoiled children who are willing to acknowledge wrongdoing but assume that God can still be counted on to make everything right. A perhaps apocryphal story is told of the free-thinking eighteenth-century philosopher Voltaire. As he was near to death, a pious friend, calling on him, suggested that it might be appropriate for him to confess his sins. "God will forgive me," Voltaire is said to have replied. "That's his job."

The people continue: "Why, O God, are you helpless, like someone after dark looking for a place to stay the night? Why are you confused, like some ineffective fighter?" (vv. 8b-9a). Here is the assemblage of the covenant community, trying to diagnose God's dysfunctions! But after all, there is no other recourse but God, and so the people end their lament by reminding God of the covenant bond: "We are called by your name, so do not leave us in the lurch!" (v. 9b).

Jeremiah relays God's answer (v. 10), and that answer is not reassuring: "The Lord does not accept them"; and the answer is reinforced by the word from Hosea, "Now he will remember their iniquity and punish their sins."

Verses 19-22, in contrast to vv. 7-9, appear to be an attempt on the people's part to dig a little deeper in their awareness of wrongdoing, to be more sincere, to try really to come to terms with what they have done. Verse 22 even reflects the effort to recite a lesson about where rain comes from; rain, they affirm, does not come from Baal, the storm god whom they sometimes worshiped (compare 2:8 and often), but from "you, O Lord our

God," upon whose mercy the people cast themselves. Nevertheless, the various approaches that the people try—"Do you really hate us?" (v. 19a); "We know we've done wrong, and our ancestors too" (v. 20); "Do not bring dishonor on yourself" (v. 21); "We've learned our lesson" (v. 22)—may still not be deep enough to satisfy God.

Now we ourselves may be uncomfortable with the notion of a close relationship between a drought and the sin of the folk who long for rain. When it comes to the question of rain, we pay more attention to the patterns of high- and low-pressure areas displayed on the screens of the evening news than we do to patterns of public and private morality. To this degree, then, the assumptions of the Bible about drought and sin may raise problems for us. On the other hand, there may loom on our own horizon a development of which Jeremiah and his people could not have conceived: our continued burning of fossil fuels, with a consequent increase of carbon dioxide in the atmosphere, may bring about global warming and *its* consequent shift in weather patterns—to that degree, then, disastrous weather in the future may be a result of our wrongdoing today.

But even if we are not so convinced that God sends drought because of our sins, we may still use occasions of public disaster to ponder our relation to the Creator; indeed, we do not need to wait for public disasters to ponder that relation.

We turn now to the parable of the Pharisee and the tax collector: it is so vivid that it will be the one on which most preachers will be impelled to concentrate. Listen to this Pharisee: "God, I thank you that I am not like other people: thieves, rogues, adulterers, or even like this tax collector. I fast twice a week; I give a tenth of all my income." Jesus has caricatured an outlook many people share. Most of us have heard the story of the fellow who heard this parable and responded with, "Well, I'm glad I'm not like that Pharisee!" It is a tricky business—even if we do not quite say, "I'm glad I'm not like those other folks," still, we may be grateful we have higher standards than many of them. The Pharisees, as we have noted, took their relation to God seriously, and self-righteousness is the besetting sin of those of us who take our relation to God seriously, because inevitably we come across people who do not seem to have any standards at all. If we avoid some of the grosser sins, we fall into others, like pride and lack of compassion.

Alongside the Pharisee, with his list of good deeds, Jesus sets the wretched tax collector who can only cry to heaven, "God, be merciful to me, a sinner!" We are assured that he is the one whom God justifies, accepts as upright, acquits of his sins. There is hope.

And we do not have to be an extortionate tax collector to voice such a cry. Not too many years ago a television reporter was interviewing Mother Teresa. In the course of the interview the reporter expressed surprise that she would have any sins at all to confess. His surprise made her laugh: "Oh, you have no idea," she said; "I have so many sins to confess every morning." This stance, a humor-filled humility, is a hard one to gain and keep.

Now one advantage of offering some interpretation of the Jeremiah passage is that it points us toward the reality of *corporate* sins; too often we are content to focus on personal sins, forgetting the whole realm of social and institutional sins. Clearly the issue for Jeremiah and his generation was the pattern of behavior of the whole covenant people, behavior shaped by the elite—ways of worship and the norms of public morality (compare Jer. 5:3-5). For them the issue was not the behavior of men and women one by one, but corporate behavior. God was judging the whole people, and as a whole they were found wanting.

Of course, one could say that the Pharisee in Jesus' parable was a representative of a whole group of teachers, and that the tax collector was part of a corrupt system of taxation, but still, each of them spoke as an individual, not as representative of a group.

We ponder then the corporate sins of our own world—the institutionalized racism and sexism, a world economy that takes little account of the needs of the poorest among us, and we wonder whether we can be any more sensitized to God's will in the face of these behaviors than Jeremiah's generation was.

Finally, let us ponder the passage from Joel. When studying the Old Testament prophets Christians sometimes ask where the prophets are these days. What they have in mind, of course, are people who stand out from the crowd, who speak for God in troubled times. To this question the passage from Joel suggests a clear answer: one should simply look around one's own congregation, for it is here, one might say, that we find the prophets of our own day. We have already noted that Peter used the passage from Joel in his Pentecost sermon to explain what the bystanders were witnessing— an outpouring of the Holy Spirit upon "all flesh," young and old, high and low, male and female. Here is the ultimate democratization of the prophetic office. No longer is the Holy Spirit confined to the rare individual; now it blankets the whole company of believers—that is to say, us, in the church.

For some congregations next Sunday will involve a celebration of Reformation Sunday, and that celebration will suggest a sermon on that memorable theme of the Reformation, the priesthood of all believers. As a preamble, here today is an opportunity for a sermon on the theme of the *prophethood* of all believers.

How are our communities of faith organized? Are women given the same status as men, as recipients of the Holy Spirit? Are young people honored as well as older folk? Is there some representation on the board of deacons for high school students, for example?

And there are wider questions too. Are public questions debated and to some degree resolved in our midst, even controversial ones? Have we learned to depersonalize controversial issues, so that it is the *issues* that we ponder and not the *people* who take one side or the other? Prophets deal with controversial issues; if the prophetic calling is one that is shared among believers, then we must explore the consequences of that calling and begin to practice it. We need to formulate at least some conclusions in the public realm, conclusions that deal with economics, and social welfare issues, and war and peace, first in order to inform ourselves and our fellow Christians, and then to help shape the wider world in which we live.

Twenty-Fourth Sunday after Pentecost
Thirty-First Sunday in Ordinary Time/Proper 26

Lectionary	First Lesson	Psalm	Second Lesson	Gospel
Revised Common	Isa. 1:10-18 or Hab. 1:1-4, 2:1-4	Ps. 32:1-7 or 119:137–144	2 Thess. 1:1-4, 11-12	Luke 19:1-10
Episcopal (BCP)	Isa. 1:10-20	Psalm 32 or 32:1-8	2 Thess. 1:1-5, (6-10), 11-12	Luke 19:1-10
Roman Catholic	Wisd. 11:22—12:1	Ps. 145:1-2, 8-11, 13-14	2 Thess. 1:11—2:2	Luke 19:1-10
Lutheran (LBW)	Exod. 34:5-9	Psalm 145	2 Thess. 1:1-5, 11-12	Luke 19:1-10

Exegesis

FIRST LESSON: ISAIAH 1:10-20

In these verses of chapter 1 we hear the clear voice of Isaiah, who spoke out during the last half of the eighth century B.C.E., announcing God's judgment on the sins of Israel. Verses 10-17 are clearly an intact sequence, a summons to receive instruction about God's disgust at the choices Israel has made, to concentrate on elaborate worship of God rather than on the observance of social justice. Verse 18, however, belongs to the following sequence, a sequence that continues through v. 20; the combination of the single v. 18 with vv. 10-17 distorts both vv. 10-17 and the meaning of v. 18 in its original context, as will be indicated by the details below.

The passage begins (v. 10) with a shock: the prophet addresses his hearers as "Sodom" and "Gomorrah," calling them by the names of the cities of old that were proverbial for wickedness (Gen. 18:16-33). It is worth a moment's pondering to imagine not only the reaction of Isaiah's hearers to this scathing identification but also the prophet's evident lack of concern for that reaction. Prophets evidently did not assume that a sympathetic hearing was a necessary ingredient in the proclamation of God's word! It is worth noting that the Hebrew word translated "teaching" in this verse is *torah*: the word of God in these verses is not simply a blast of the moment but "teaching," "law," the steady word of guidance for the behavior of the covenant people.

Verses 11-14 refer to details of the public worship of Israel, which was centered in sacrifice. Verse 11 opens with God's rhetorical question, "What to me is the multitude of your sacrifices?" and then continues with a listing

TWENTY-FOURTH SUNDAY AFTER PENTECOST/PROPER 26   37

of the fat and blood of various beasts for which God has no craving. And vv. 13 and 14 go on to mention incense offerings and festivals.

This prophetic rejection of sacrifice raises the question of the attitude in the Old Testament toward animal sacrifice in worship: was it considered a good thing or a bad thing? This is not the only passage in which the prophets appear to reject sacrifice: one thinks of Amos 5:21-24 and Mic. 6:6-8, among others. On the other hand, laws set forth in Leviticus and elsewhere certainly assume without question the centrality of animal sacrifice in Israel's worship. Perhaps we would be on the right track by understanding the prophets to proclaim a *priority*: social justice is *more* important than sacrifice.

Verse 10 is thus not the only shock in the passage. Look at the emotional words from God in vv. 11-14: "I have had enough"(v. 11); "[incense is] an abomination to me," "I cannot endure" (v. 13); "my soul hates," "I am weary" (v. 14)! Isaiah perceives God really to be disgusted.

Verse 15 is a transitional verse: "When you stretch out your hands [in prayer], I will hide my eyes from you." God will no longer hear the people's prayers. Why? "Your hands are full of blood." And then vv. 16 and 17 offer an avalanche of commands, which are even more abrupt in Hebrew than in English; in the original language it sounds roughly like, "Wash, clean up, take the evil of your deeds from my eyes, stop evil, learn good, seek justice, save the poor, defend orphans, help widows." Here, reduced to the simplest terms, are the commands to do justice.

Verses 10-17, then, reflect in the strongest terms God's rejection of the practices of Israel's worship. And if God is no longer willing to hear the prayers of the people, the impression one gains is that Isaiah understands God to reject any possibility of the people's change of heart.

We turn now to v. 18. This verse, which picks up the motif of "blood" from the end of v. 15, appears in the usual translations to affirm that no matter how grievous one's sins may be, they can be wiped away, and in this understanding the verse has been the theme of much gospel preaching. But this verse, as has already been stated, begins a new sequence that actually ends with v. 20 and must be understood in the light of the two alternatives presented in vv. 19-20: "If you are . . . obedient, you shall eat the good of the land, but if you . . . rebel, you shall be devoured by the sword." And because v. 18 has to be heard in the light of the two alternatives in vv. 19-20, there has been strong opinion among many commentators for the last two centuries that v. 18 poses not positive affirmations but rather *rhetorical questions*. So reads the translation of Alex R. Gordon in *The American Bible, A Complete Translation* (1939): "If your sins be like scarlet, can they become white as snow? If they be red like crimson, can they become as wool?" One recent commentator has even taken the words of this verse as scornful sarcasm. By this understanding, then, does God entertain the possibility in v. 18 that the people's heart will change? Clearly yes, *but not unconditionally*: the people must be obedient in order for God to accept them back.

How can we understand the contrast of perspective between vv. 10-17 and v. 18? One could imagine vv. 10-17 having been proclaimed at the beginning of Isaiah's career: his understanding of God's will at the time of his call was dark indeed (compare 6:9-10); vv. 18-20, by contrast, may reflect a more moderate outlook later in his career. We cannot know for sure. But what is clear is that when we link v. 18 to vv. 10-17, when we cut off the lesson at the end of v. 18, and when we assume that v. 18 offers without question an unconditional promise of forgiveness, we are distorting to some degree the words of Isaiah.

(For Habakkuk 1:1-4; 2:2-4, see the first lesson for the Twentieth Sunday after Pentecost.)

SECOND LESSON: 2 THESSALONIANS 1:1-4, 11-12

Though *First* Thessalonians is clearly authentic to Paul, it is likely that Second Thessalonians is not, but is rather a later work sent out in Paul's name; there are clear differences of perspective between the two letters. For example, in First Thessalonians Paul urges vigilance in preparation for Christ's early return (1 Thess. 5:1-11), whereas in Second Thessalonians the last judgment is painted in grimmer colors (2 Thess. 1:5-10). And the reference in 2 Thess. 2:2 to false reports, perhaps in a previous letter, suggests that the work is an attempt to counter a misunderstanding of Paul (see discussion of this matter in the exegesis of the second lesson for next Sunday). So in spite of the insistence in 2 Thess. 3:17 on Paul's authorship, we would do well to understand the letter as a pseudonymous work from roughly the end of the first century C.E.

The lesson today begins with verses from the opening thanksgiving of the letter. Verses 1-4 embody the address and greeting (vv. 1-2), followed by the author's thanksgiving for the faith and love of the recipients. Then vv. 11-12 are an affirmation that the writer offers constant prayer for God's blessing on the readers. It is God who extends the grace that will make the faithful worthy of God's call.

GOSPEL: LUKE 19:1-10

The readings in the lectionary pass over Luke 18:15-43; we arrive today at the narrative of Zacchaeus. This narrative, like the healing in 17:11-19 and the parables in 18:1-8 and 9-14, is unique to Luke. It is the second incident associated with Jericho, the first having been the healing of a blind man (18:35-43), an incident taken from Mark (see Mark 10:46-52 and Matt. 20:29-34).

The first verse sets the stage; the incident proper is contained in vv. 2-9, and v. 10 appears to be the kind of tagline that was secondarily associated with the narrative—it is found in some manuscripts of Matt. 18:11 (see the NRSV margin there) and is a variation of Luke 5:32.

One may raise a further question about v. 8, since Jesus' statement in v. 9 really follows not on v. 8 at all but rather on the crowd's murmuring back in v. 7: the "salvation" that "has come to this house" (v. 9) is not brought about by Zacchaeus's giving up of much of his wealth, but rather by the visit of Jesus. One wonders, then, whether v. 8 is not an addition to the tradition, perhaps inserted by Luke himself.

It is useful here to recall the remarks concerning tax collectors in the exegesis of last week's Gospel. Jericho was a border town, so there would have been an important tax station there. And Zacchaeus was not simply a tax collector, but a chief of tax collectors: "[he] was rich" (v. 2). Since he had greater access to the profits within the taxation system, people would have hated him all the more. His name was a common one at the time (compare the name of the leader of the Pharisees at the end of the first century C.E., Johanan ben *Zakkai*), but since the name means "pure, righteous," the contrast between the meaning of his name and the office he held would have been appalling to his fellows. And, a humorous touch: he was not very tall (vv. 3-4). Clearly, then, he was not someone whom even compassionate people would be impelled to respect.

With regard to v. 8, it is important to know that Zacchaeus's giving one-half to the poor was voluntary: there was no regulation in Jewish law on the matter. But his return fourfold of money taken by fraud is an elaboration derived from the regulation for stealing a sheep in Exod. 22:1. The overall implication of this verse gives trouble, however, since we are uncertain whether the present-tense verbs in Greek imply *customary* behavior (RSV: "I give," "I restore"; compare the implication of "I give" in 18:12) or imply *new* behavior in the future (NRSV: "I will give," "I will pay back"). Is Zacchaeus to be understood as defending his customary behavior, or is he announcing a change of style of life because of his new relation to Jesus? It is striking that Jesus offers no pronouncement of *forgiveness* to Zacchaeus;

rather, he vindicates the tax collector to the crowd. Part of the problem here is our modern notion that Jesus' approval of Zaccheus must be related to a *conversion*. It may be then that the RSV is correct after all, and that Jesus here is defending the *steady behavior* of Zacchaeus.

Homiletical Interpretation

As in earlier weeks, we find it difficult to relate the second lesson to the other two; the passage from 2 Thessalonians appears simply to offer a backdrop of general approval of Christian character. And we find it equally difficult to relate the lesson from Habakkuk to the passage from Luke; suggestions for dealing with the Habakkuk passage may be found in the homiletical interpretation for the Twentieth Sunday after Pentecost.

This leaves the passages from Isaiah and Luke. If one adopts a traditional approach to both passages—that, in regard to Isa. 1:18, it serves as the climax to the previous eight verses, and proclaims the possibility of God's forgiveness, no matter how serious one's sins have been, and that, in regard to the passage from Luke, the episode involves Zacchaeus's repentance from his sins—then the way is open to preach both repentance and a new life in the gospel in the fashion that has been expressed so often, and often so well. But the remarks in the exegesis section on both passages raise enough doubts about that traditional approach that one might consider other understandings of one or both passages. First let us stay with the possibility of treating both texts in the same sermon.

One possibility is to contrast the morality of groups with the morality of individuals (compare the suggestion for a comparison of the Jeremiah passage with the passage from Luke for the Twenty-Third Sunday after Pentecost). The Isaiah passage deals collectively with the nation of Israel and with God's abhorrence of the behavior of the nation, behavior centered on the ever-more elaborate public worship that the nation observed, to the detriment of elementary justice. These patterns of worship were institutionalized, and it is extraordinarily difficult to change the behavior of institutions. It is hard enough for individuals to change, but, by comparison, institutions resist change far more keenly, a matter explored a half-century ago by Reinhold Niebuhr in his book *Moral Man and Immoral Society*. If one assumes that Zacchaeus underwent an experience of conversion, then the way is open to lay the two passages side by side: in Isaiah's day God pondered the unlikely possibility that Israel could shift its priorities, while centuries later, in Jesus' day, Zacchaeus did accept a new set of priorities.

Let us now ponder a sermon that concentrates on the passage from Isaiah. Verses 10-17 appear to forbid any investment by the covenant community in elaborate worship; God's sole concern, it would seem, is social justice. Congregations today face constant choices. Should X dollars be invested in repair of the organ or contributed to the budget of a local shelter for the homeless? The words from Isaiah simply underline such dilemmas. As the remarks in the exegesis section suggest, it is unlikely that Isaiah envisages the total abolition of the rites of public worship. It is inconceivable that he had in mind some ancient equivalent of a Quaker silent meeting for worship, with no set liturgy or rites; the suggestion I offer is that it was a matter of priorities. Jesus is remembered as making the matter explicit: "First be reconciled to your brother or sister, and then come and offer your gift" (Matt. 5:24). Christian churches have three obligations—to worship God, to deepen community, and to do justice. The text from Isaiah reminds us that one obligation cannot exclude another.

The problem is, of course, that it is always a temptation to elaborate our architecture, to bring more beauty into our worship, to add even more special features to our celebrations of Christmas and Easter than we have had heretofore. It is a fine line between the honoring of God and God's mighty acts on the one hand and the public display of our skills and treasure on the other. Social justice is rarely so exciting: it demands hard work, stubborn staying power, and involves us in controversy. It is useful, therefore, to feel the cold water God throws in our faces through the words of Isaiah.

Now how might a sermon go that concentrates on the Gospel lesson? It is worth noting that Jesus' last word is to the crowd, not to Zacchaeus. "Today salvation has come to this house, because he too is a son of Abraham." Galatians 3:29 does not apply here: Zacchaeus *has not become* a son of Abraham in some spiritual sense, rather he *already is* a son of Abraham, a fellow-Jew. Jesus chose a hated rich man, one regarded as a sinner and a traitor, as his host!

We need to be reminded of the central importance of hospitality in the whole complex of honor and shame that is central to the biblical world. For us the role of host and hostess for a dinner party is too often construed as obligation; in the eastern Mediterranean world, by contrast, it is considered an honor to be the host. In the story of the prodigal son, the older son refused to go in to greet the guests (Luke 15:28); he thus dishonored both his father and the guests. In Lebanon today the Arabic greeting to a guest is always *tsharrafna*, "you honor us." In the eyes of the crowd Zacchaeus had lived in shame; now a guest has honored him, and, in the eyes of the crowd, Jesus is a noteworthy guest indeed. Of course in the tradition of the story that came down through Christian circles, Jesus is the Savior. "Today salvation has come to this house." But one must not forget that that salvation came through the honoring of a host who had theretofore been despised.

Wonderful questions of ethics come to mind. What is God's judgment, and ours, on a person who makes a living in a socially disapproved way but is generous in private benefactions? What is God's judgment, and ours, when we rarely see more than an individual's outer behavior, whereas God knows his or her inner attitude? Indeed, how are we to understand God's judgment at all alongside human judgment? The old expression, *vox populi vox Dei*, "the voice of the people is the voice of God," may encourage the day-to-day decisions we need to make within the compromises of a political democracy, but from the biblical perspective it is hardly the ultimate truth.

And if one wants to press the conclusion, discussed in the exegesis section but unexpected to most hearers, that Zacchaeus was that surprising phenomenon, a good and thoughtful chief tax collector within a rotten system of taxation, then one has a remarkable opportunity to watch Jesus defending someone whom the crowd has rejected out of prejudice. One could find any number of modern examples of individuals whom Christians need to defend against the thoughtless opinion of the crowds; needless to say, however, when we cite such modern examples, we will court the disapproval of folk in our congregations who have already made up their minds.

Whatever we make of the episode of Zacchaeus, it is clear that Jesus consorted with all sorts of people and thus broke the conventional boundaries of acceptable social behavior among his fellow Jews. He thus continues to challenge our facile assessment of our fellows and our behavior toward them.

Twenty-Fifth Sunday after Pentecost
Thirty-Second Sunday in Ordinary Time/Proper 27

Lectionary	First Lesson	Psalm	Second Lesson	Gospel
Revised Common	Job 19:23-27a or Hag. 1:15b—2:9	Ps. 17:1-9 or 145:1-5, 17-21 or Ps. 98	2 Thess. 2:1-5, 13-17	Luke 20:27-38
Episcopal (BCP)	Job 19:23-27a	Psalm 17 or 17:1-8	2 Thess. 2:13—3:5	Luke 20:27, (28-33), 34-38
Roman Catholic	2 Macc. 7:1-2, 9-14	Ps. 17:1, 5-6, 8, 15	2 Thess. 2:16—3:5	Luke 20:27-38 or Luke 20:27, 34-38
Lutheran (LBW)	1 Chron. 29:10-13	Psalm 148	2 Thess. 2:13—3:5	Luke 20:27-38

Exegesis

FIRST LESSON: JOB 19:23-27a

In the course of the poetic portion of the book of Job one will have heard Job's initial lament (chapter 3), the whole first cycle of the speeches of Job's friends and Job's reply to each (chapters 4–14), and a portion of the second cycle (Eliphaz's speech, Job's reply, and Bildad's speech, chapters 15–18). Chapter 19 contains Job's reply to Bildad in that cycle, so the verses in today's lesson form part of that reply.

In vv. 2-5 of that chapter Job addresses his friends ("you" there is plural); he complains of their shabby treatment, as he has in previous passages (see 8:2). In vv. 6-12 Job affirms that God is his enemy; God attacks Job as if the latter were a city under siege. In vv. 13-20 he offers a catalog of those in his household and his circle of associates who have rejected him; he is a social isolate, even from his wife (v. 17).

Verses 21-29 form the climax of the chapter. It is striking that the verses expressing hope that make up the lesson are enclosed by two negative sequences, vv. 21-22 and vv. 28-29: vv. 21 and 29 contain imperatives of warning to his friends ("have pity on me," "fear the sword"), and vv. 22 and 28 are indictments of his friends, who "pursue" him ("persecute" in v. 28 is the same word). Job cannot count on them.

Verses 23-24 may express hope, but it is a wan hope, a vain wish, really, that his legal case against God might be on a public record for posterity forever. It would be gratifying, he thinks, to be vindicated after his death, but then it will hardly do him any good!

Verses 25-27a, the two-and-a-half verses to which we are so attracted, bristle, alas, with difficulties (note the no less than six text notes in the

NRSV). It would be nice to keep it simple, staying with the aria from *Messiah*, "I know that my Redeemer liveth," but the details are not so simple.

Verse 25 should begin "But I know" (so the *Revised English Bible*); Job's affirmation is based neither on the support of his friends nor the survival of any public record of his case. He knows, he says, that his *go'el* is living. What does this Hebrew word mean? It has not occurred earlier in the book, but in 9:33 Job expresses the wish that there might be an *umpire* between himself and God, and in 16:19 he speaks of a *witness* in heaven who can vouch for him and intercede for him: clearly in these passsages the "umpire" or "witness" is someone other than God. So here: the *go'el* is not God, as some folk have assumed, but rather a vindicator before God. Job is convinced that there must be a figure who can defend him in heaven.

We turn now to the details of the sequence. There are many uncertainties in our understanding of the next four lines. The repetitions and the odd word order suggest high emotion. Let us try this, for a translation: "[25] But I myself am convinced that my [heavenly] vindicator [a member of the divine council?] is living, and that afterward [that is, after my death] he will rise up [to defend me in court] upon the dust [of my grave, or of Sheol (the abode of the dead)], [26] that is, after my skin has peeled off; and [thus] from my flesh [that is, personally] I will behold God, [27] whom I myself will behold for my own sake, and it is my eyes that see, not someone else's." In this understanding Job is convinced that he will finally be face to face with his great adversary, God (compare his hope in 13:15), and thus gain vindication.

Though these words have become precious to English-speaking Christians in the wording of the KJV, it is important to keep in mind both the difficulties of understanding the immediate four-and-a-half verses, and the context in which the words appear—Job's hope-against-hope to maintain his integrity in the face of the monstrous treatment he has undergone at the hands of God.

ALTERNATIVE FIRST LESSON: HAGGAI 1:15b—2:9

The book of Haggai consists of five addresses dated to 520 B.C.E., of which this is the second. Jews had returned from Babylon to Jerusalem after the exile, and work has been renewed on the rebuilding of the temple. In the passage under discussion Haggai assures his listeners that the new structure will be more splendid than the old.

Now we learn from Ezra 3:10-13, a passage referring to the same historical moment, that at the time the foundations of the new temple were laid, while many folk were overjoyed, some, who could remember the old temple, wept. One is left then with the impression that there were some folk who doubted that the new temple would be so grand as the earlier structure had been. To the contrary, says Haggai; God will see to its glory. After all, God was with the people when they were brought out of Egypt (v. 5). Indeed, God will soon shake the heavens and the earth (v. 6). This is an expression often used for God's judgment in political turmoil—the reference is doubtless to the turmoil accompanying the accession of the Persian king Darius to the throne the previous year. God will bring back the treasure of the nations (by implication these will include the treasure looted from the old temple) so that the new temple will be filled with splendor, and other nations will acknowledge the power of the God of Israel. Haggai's point, of course, is that now and always God is the chief actor in history.

SECOND LESSON: 2 THESSALONIANS 2:1-5, 13-17

Verses 1-5 and 13-17 of this chapter do not cohere with each other too well, so that it is better to discuss the two passages separately.

Verses 1-5 of the lesson affirm that the day of the Lord is not yet here. We are back in a world in which Christians were deeply divided on basic matters of belief. The passage may have reference to those who follow the belief of those in Johannine circles, who affirmed that there is *no* future last judgment. Thus in John 5:24 one has, "Very truly, I tell you, anyone who hears my word and believes him who sent me has eternal life, and does not come under judgment, but has passed from death to life" (compare 1 John 3:14). On the other hand, these verses may have reference to people led astray by men who identified themselves as Christ returned (compare the warning in Mark 13:6). In any event it is likely that the author, by drafting this letter over the name of Paul, is trying to counter a misinterpretation of the word that Paul had written in 1 Thess. 4:13—5:11. The writer appeals for calm (v. 2), stating that various signs of the end time must come before the day of the Lord (v. 3), such as widespread apostasy (compare Matt. 24:9-14) and the coming of an anti-Christ figure.

Verses 13-17 embody a thanksgiving for God's call to the recipients (vv. 13-15) and a prayer that they stay firm in the faith (vv. 16-17). These sentiments are hardly different from those in the second lesson for the Twenty-Fourth Sunday after Pentecost.

GOSPEL: LUKE 20:27-38

This incident, of the Sadducees' questioning Jesus about the resurrection of the dead, is part of the tradition of events that took place after Jesus entered Jerusalem. The narrative is found in all three Synoptic Gospels, so that the source is Mark.

Two matters need to be kept in mind with regard to the belief in resurrection in the Bible. The first is that in the Old Testament a conviction about resurrection was largely lacking; the general Old Testament assumption is that one lived on in one's children. Thus God promised Jacob that he would spread out to all four points of the compass, that is, in his offspring (Gen. 28:14); and when God called Jeremiah to celibacy (Jer. 16:1-4), it is a calling to his extinction, as a symbol for the extinction of the nation. It is true, during the Babylonian exile the prophet Ezekiel offered a vision of the revivification of the dry bones as a picture of the revivification of the nation (Ezek. 37:1-14), but this was national renewal rather than personal resurrection. On the other hand, as the decades passed, the constant experience of righteous Jews who died without any vindication at all pressed on them an urgency to solve the riddle of where God's justice might be found, and the notion of resurrection began to be thought of as a solution to the riddle. There is a late passage, Isa. 26:16-19, that suggests that the righteous will surely be raised to life once more, though that passage offers several difficulties in interpretation. It is only in the intertestamental books (the Apocrypha) that one sees the notion of resurrection really taking hold—one notable passage is 2 Maccabees 7, a narrative of the martyrdom of seven brothers and their mother, each of whom died affirming the reality of the resurrection.

The second matter to be kept in mind is the necessity to make a distinction between the Jewish notion of *resurrection*, that is, God's raising of persons from the dead, and the Greek notion of *immortality*, the idea that persons, or at least righteous persons, continue in some way to live after physical death. The Greek notion began to affect Jewish ideas, and one sees evidence for a belief in immortality in some passages in the Apocrypha; for example, Wis. 1:12-15 affirms that God has made human beings for immortality. But the circles in which Jesus moved were not touched deeply touched by Greek ideas.

These circles were dominated by the Pharisees, who, as we have seen, developed notions in oral law that attempted to be open to emerging religious issues (see the exegesis of the Gospel for the Twenty-Third Sunday after Pentecost). By contrast, the Sadducees were a priestly, aristocratic party centered in the Jerusalem temple, and, as v. 27 affirms, they denied the resurrection, holding to a strict interpretation of written Torah. (The disagreement between the Pharisees and the Sadducees over the question of resurrection was the basis, we recall, of Paul's self-defense before the Council in Jerusalem, recorded in Acts 23:6-8.)

The Sadducees offered Jesus an absurd hypothetical question; indeed, it was perhaps the stock question regarding the resurrection posed by Sadducees to Pharisees. But if the Sadducees' question was originally framed to ridicule the Pharisees' belief in the resurrection, this narrative must have delighted the followers of Jesus, who saw the Sadducees' attempt at ridicule backfire when their question was posed to the Master.

The question was based on the old Jewish law of levirate marriage (Deut. 25:5-6), by which, if a man died without having produced a son, his brother would be obligated to marry the widow and produce a son to carry on the name of the dead man and maintain his property within that line of the family as well (this is the situation presumed in the story of Onan in Gen. 38:8). So the Sadducees pose their question: an utterly luckless woman married seven successive brothers without producing a child; whose wife will she then be in the resurrection? Jesus' answer is that marriage and consequent procreation are matters for "this age" but are not necessary in the world to come. Then he buttresses his teaching by reference to Exod. 3:6, whose authority the Sadducees would certainly accept; he finds an implicit reference to the resurrection there, since Moses speaks of the patriarchs as living (and therefore resurrected). To him it is plain that the dead do not have a God.

Homiletical Interpretation

The reading from Haggai is related to the Gospel only in the general sense that God is affirmed to be the author of history and will therefore take care of the righteous in the future. Most preachers will prefer the reading from Job, since one can see ways to relate it directly to Jesus' debate with the Sadducees.

If the exegesis of Job given above is sound, then Job is affirming his conviction, beyond any immediate evidence, that he will gain a final legal victory with the aid of his heavenly vindicator. It is important to note that Job's problem is not survival or life after death in and of itself; his problem is vindication. The passage then centers on that issue, even though Job is unable to envisage his vindication, even after death, without somehow being able to see it for himself. As we have seen, his conviction that he will ultimately be vindicated is extravagant in the context of the total book. Nevertheless, from the vantage point of the faith that Christians have in Christ the Redeemer, that faith both reinforces Job's belief in ultimate vindication and is reinforced by the passage in Job.

By the same token the memory of Jesus' encounter with the Sadducees is mightily shaped, in the faith of the believing community, by the centrality of Christ's own resurrection (compare 1 Cor. 15:12-14). So in this passage we can see Jesus, whom we know to be our Redeemer, besting the Sadducees and their silly riddle, while we are aware that in less than a week he will himself be resurrected.

Now modern Christians in many faith communities affirm their faith by their recitation of the Apostles' Creed, which includes the affirmation, "I believe in the resurrection of the dead." This affirmation is squarely based on passages in the New Testament, such as 1 Cor. 15:52, which proclaim the raising of the dead at the last trumpet.

On the other hand, it is clear that our own sensibilities today with regard to life beyond the grave are shaped not only by such affirmations of resurrection but also by counter-pressures from the culture in which we live. One of them is the practice of cremation, a practice that subtly undermines ideas we have about the raising of the dead. Beyond this particular matter, there are more substantial counter-pressures. Let us note a few.

First, our culture is dominated by a naturalistic, scientific worldview that challenges any beliefs not based on evidence that can be photographed and measured. By this view, death not only marks the end of physical life but is assumed to mark the end of personal survival as well.

Second, since it is utterly natural to crave some kind of survival after death, most people hold to some such belief. For some folk this belief is based on an idealistic notion of the survival of the "soul," thought of as a nonphysical essence of identity: this notion is akin to the ancient Greek notion of immortality. Such idealism may be reinforced by notions derived from Eastern religions, or from various popular "new age" movements.

Third, the belief in the survival of the "soul" may be reinforced by what is affirmed or assumed in most Christian funeral services. It is widely thought that the deceased go immediately on death to be in the presence of God, in the presence of Jesus, and in the presence of formerly deceased members of their family and friends. The urge to be reunited with our loved ones immediately after death is deep indeed, but it cuts across the belief in resurrection at the time of a future last judgment.

Fourth, the weakening of the ideas of the last judgment, of the punishment of the wicked, and of hell (except as a vehicle for jokes and rude language), has shifted the moral urgencies of the biblical belief.

All this is complicated by our common avoidance of any easy discussion of death. The result is that we rarely talk about death except at times when death threatens us, or those close to us, or when death has taken someone close to us—that is, occasions when we are emotionally most vulnerable. And thus our thinking is not coherent but very much in a muddle.

So, we begin with God. God has loved us into being; God is beyond space and time, and God will take care of us beyond space and time. God has signaled this to us in sending Jesus to live out this care for us even to his death, death on a cross, and in raising Jesus to life forever. The biblical way this is expressed is anticipated in the passage in Job and is affirmed without question by Jesus in the Gospel lesson, the trustworthiness of our conviction of the resurrection of the dead.

Of course, no one now living has any firsthand experience with what lies beyond death, but Christians are able to affirm the word in Heb. 11:1, "Now faith is the assurance of things hoped for, the conviction of things not seen." And there is another word in Hebrews, "Therefore, since we are surrounded by so great a cloud of witnesses, let us also lay aside every weight and the sin that clings so closely, and let us run with perseverance the race that is set before us, looking to Jesus the pioneer and perfecter of our faith, who for the sake of the joy that was set before him endured the cross, disregarding its shame, and has taken his seat at the right hand of the throne of God" (Heb. 12:1-2).

Our dread of death can be a weight that clings closely indeed; but we are enabled to throw it off in part by the company of that great cloud of witnesses. Every congregation has a cloud of witnesses, folk who have borne suffering and pain and loss with dignity and grace and even humor. Every congregation has its saints who give us courage to run the race that is set before us. The writer of the second lesson today can speak of "eternal comfort and good hope" (2 Thess. 2:16).

The Sadducees thought the notion of resurrection was ridiculous. We still have Sadducees in our midst. But Jesus knew better, and so may we.

Twenty-Sixth Sunday after Pentecost
Thirty-Third Sunday in Ordinary Time/Proper 28

Lectionary	First Lesson	Psalm	Second Lesson	Gospel
Revised Common	Mal. 4:1-2a or Isa. 65:17-25	Psalm 98 or Isaiah 12	2 Thess. 3:6-13	Luke 21:5-19
Episcopal (BCP)	Mal. 3:13—4:2a, 5-6	Psalm 98 or 98:5-10	2 Thess. 3:6-13	Luke 21:5-19
Roman Catholic	Mal. 4:1-2a	Ps. 98:5-9	2 Thess. 3:7-12	Luke 21:5-19
Lutheran (LBW)	Mal. 4:1-2a	Psalm 98	2 Thess. 3:6-13	Luke 21:5-19

Exegesis

FIRST LESSON: MALACHI 4:1-2a

The book of Malachi comes from a time well along in the postexilic period, perhaps in the decades before Nehemiah, whose career can be dated to about 445 B.C.E. It offers a series of disputations: typically the prophet sets forth an address of God to the people, then cites the people's words, then cites God's answer (see, for example, 3:13-18). It is a time of slack religion: the people maintained that it does no good to serve God, since evildoers prosper (3:14-15).

The verse-and-a-half in the reading are part of God's correction of such slackness. God affirms that there will be a day of judgment in which evildoers will be burned like stubble, while those who revere God will bask under the "sun of righteousness" (for this phrase compare Ps. 84:11).

ALTERNATIVE FIRST LESSON: ISAIAH 65:17-25

In contrast to the passage from Malachi, this one is altogether reassuring. The prophet (whom commentators often call "Third Isaiah") wrote during the period 520–515 B.C.E. He envisages "new heavens and a new earth" (v. 17) and is thus urging on his hearers an expectation of an apocalyptic shift in the order of things. In this shift God will answer the prayers of the people even before they have a chance to voice them (v. 24). The prophet looks forward to the rejoicing of Jerusalem (vv. 18-19), an end to infant mortality and indeed to any premature death (v. 20), and an end to the alienation of one's property by an oppressor (vv. 21-22).

The mortality rate must have been high indeed in those days, though there is no way of course to know how high. But archaeological expeditions have laid bare the layout of houses, and it is clear that people lived in close quarters to each other. Winters would be damp and cold, and water supplies could be contaminated. Recurrent infectious diseases and occasional plagues must have taken a high toll.

Foreign conquerors could be expected to take over one's lands and other property; the book of Jeremiah has vivid descriptions of this expectation (see Jer. 4:16; 5:17). And one could suffer expropriation of one's property from a fellow Israelite for nonpayment of debt (see Jer. 5:26-28).

Verse 25, a summary of 11:6-9, foresees the end of the threat of hurtful animals: wolf and lamb shall feed together, and the lion shall eat straw.

SECOND LESSON: 2 THESSALONIANS 3:6-13

This passage is a sturdy warning against idleness. In v. 6 the KJV refers to "every brother that walketh disorderly," and the Greek adverb that occurs here, *ataktos,* describes undisciplined behavior: it was frequently used to describe the actions of soldiers who broke ranks. The *New Jerusalem Bible,* in this passage, speaks of those who live "an undisciplined life." Yet it is clear from the references in the following three verses to Paul's steady work that the question of discipline involved the question of *work*—being about one's own business rather than involving oneself in the business of others (v. 11).

One may wonder whether this warning did not emerge because of the conviction on the part of many that the day of the Lord was at hand (or had already arrived). Such a conviction would have encouraged "loafing." On the other hand, we all know how easily a radical religious movement may attract odd and irresponsible folk who then exploit the excitement that the movement engenders. In the present passage there are reminiscences of Gen. 3:17-19, the word to the first man, that he must eat bread by the sweat of his face. One can then imagine the behavior of converts, perhaps coming out of Hellenistic paganism, for whom such Jewish norms were unfamiliar. In any event the injunction, "Anyone unwilling to work should not eat," is stern enough to suggest that there was a real problem in the circles to which the letter was directed.

GOSPEL: LUKE 21:5-19

This selection is the first section of Luke's version of the so-called "Synoptic Apocalypse," which continues through v. 36; the portion selected for the Gospel today is Luke's adaptation of Mark 13:1-13. Jesus is portrayed as predicting the destruction of the temple, vv. 5-6, describing the signs of the end time (vv. 8-11), and then referring to the troubles the disciples will undergo (vv. 12-19).

The historical Jesus doubtless offered his disciples many indications of a coming destruction of Jerusalem, but there is also no doubt that the Gospel of Mark arranged and heightened those indications in the context of the terrible Roman–Jewish War of 68-70 C.E. And Luke in turn has touched up the wording of Mark: for example, v. 18 is an addition of Luke's. But since there is no way convincingly to tease out of this passage any plausible reconstruction of the original words of the historical Jesus, it is safer simply to take the passage as a reflection of the understanding of Jesus' words about the events of the fall of Jerusalem in 70 C.E. by Christians at the end of the first century, in the light of their expectation of the end of the age.

Verses 5-7 concern the immediate fate of the temple. This building in its essentials was in continuity with the temple rebuilt and completed about 515 B.C.E. (see the discussion on Hag. 2:3 in the exegesis for the Twenty-Fifth Sunday after Pentecost). That temple may have been modest in its proportions, but it was enlarged and beautified by Herod the Great, beginning about 20 B.C.E.; the Jewish historian Josephus describes the "hard white stones" and the covering of "massive plates of gold," so that the pride of the bystanders in the temple (v. 5) is understandable. The expression attributed to Jesus, "not one stone upon another," is a set phrase (see 19:44), but Josephus's description of the ruin of Jerusalem by 70 C.E. indicates that the phrase was not much of an exaggeration. From the biblical point of view, these words would remind hearers of earlier prophetic words, such as that "Jerusalem shall become a heap of ruins" (Mic. 3:12).

The disciples' question, "When will this be?" (v. 7), leads to the apocalyptic discourse proper; the following verses in the lesson divide into two—vv. 8-11, the signs before the end of Jerusalem, and vv. 12-19, admonitions for the coming persecution.

Verse 8 warns of the coming of false prophets, of whom there were many in those decades: we find references to Theudas in Acts 5:36 and to an unnamed Egyptian in Acts 21:38. There would even be those who would identify themselves as Jesus returned! Verses 9-10 speak of wars and insurrections; these were a standard ingredient in apocalyptic descriptions (compare Zech. 14:2; Dan. 11:25, 44). In v. 9 "the end" refers to the end of Jerusalem, not to the end of the world. Again earthquakes and famines were a standard part of apocalyptic predictions (for earthquakes compare Hag. 2:6); and we note that in the book of Acts Luke mentions an earthquake when Paul and Silas were imprisoned in Philippi (Acts 16:26) and a famine under the emperor Claudius (Acts 11:28).

The admonitions in vv. 12-19 reassure the hearers at the end of the first century that the persecutions suffered by Christians were already predicted by Jesus and therefore altogether to be expected. These persecutions will come from both Jewish and Gentile authorities (v. 12); they will be occasions to testify to the faith (v. 13). Jesus' followers must not be concerned about the defense they will make, because Jesus himself will give them the words they need (v. 15; we may note in passing that Luke insists it is Jesus himself who will do this, not the Holy Spirit, as Mark 13:11 has it). The persecutions will come not only from external authorities but even from one's own friends and family, and some will suffer death (v. 16); Luke narrates in the book of Acts the martyrdoms of Stephen and of James the son of Zebedee (Acts 7:54; 12:1-2). Note that in v. 17 the phrase "because of my name" is repeated from v. 12. "Not a hair on your head will perish" (v. 18) is an echo of 12:7; by endurance you will "gain your souls" (that is, procure [real, that is, eternal] life). The Greek word translated "soul" here, *psyche*, is translated "life" in a similar context in 9:24.

Homiletical Interpretation

As the end of the church year approaches, it is appropriate to think about last things: not the last moment in the earthly life of each individual, nor one's vision of eternal bliss, but the culmination, in the work of God, of history, of the public affairs of men and women and of nations. To this end one has for this day two alternative Old Testament depictions, one, from Malachi, which could lead to trepidation, and the other, portraying only hope, from the book of Isaiah. Given these two, most preachers will probably gravitate to Isaiah. Yet one should not turn away from Malachi too soon. Though the accent in that passage is on "you who revere my name" (v. 2), it describes the fate of the arrogant and all evildoers as well. Since we have all met and perhaps even suffered under folk who are arrogant evildoers, who too often prevail for as long as we can imagine, it is reassuring to hear that ultimately they will be treated like stubble. John the Baptist was later remembered as insisting that the Messiah will gather the wheat into the granary but will burn the chaff with unquenchable fire (Luke 3:17), so this vision is not singular to Malachi.

The reading from Isaiah 65, as already noted, sets forth a vision of a future for the redeemed Jerusalem. For us today the passage may evoke two rather contrary reactions. The first is a sense of incongruity, in that it links together what to us is impossible as the world now is, namely the metamorphosis of carnivorous animals into herbivores, with what is quite conceivable to us in the world as it is, namely the reduction of mortality rates and the abolition of expropriation of property. In Europe and North America, in our day, medical innovations and public health measures have reduced infant mortality to a marvelous degree; the life span of more and more individuals extends years beyond the seventy or eighty proclaimed by the psalmist (Ps. 90:10). And again, few in our congregations have experienced a loss of property to foreign conquerors, and any domestic expropriation proceeds within the context of law. Our local Jerusalems do experience joy, over and over again; it is a gift that we have really experienced.

The second reaction is an identification with these folk twenty-six hundred years ago. The passage opens to us a window into the poignancy of human despair in the face of the losses people have sustained within the compass of their lives, a poignancy with which we, out of our own experience, can identify directly. If infant mortality has been reduced and life has been extended for many in our midst, nevertheless this reality is no comfort to those parents who grieve over babies who have died, no comfort to those stunned when cherished members of their families or circles of friends die "before their time." And if we ourselves have not had snatched from our hands the houses we have built and the trees we have planted, we can certainly empathize with those who experience such losses.

And indeed, there are wide swaths of the world where people's vulnerability to disease, or to the expropriation of property, or to victimization by violence, prevails in ways no different from the situation twenty-six hundred years ago, except for the fact that the weapons available to the violent are so much deadlier in our day. We are vividly reminded by the images of evening news that millions of folk experience losses like these before our very eyes. We live in the century of the refugee.

The passage in Isaiah describes, then, that gift of God, the peaceable kingdom, where we are assured that all will be well in our lives, where wolf and lamb shall feed together. It is a gift that we await with eagerness, given the ocean of tears shed in the course of human history.

Now if the passage from Malachi speaks both of the destruction of those who oppose God and of the reward of those who are loyal to God in the time to come, and if the passage from Isaiah speaks only of the reward of those who are loyal to God, then the passage from Luke speaks of the agony undergone by those who are loyal to Jesus Christ in the time before the end. We turn then to the lessons from the New Testament.

TWENTY-SIXTH SUNDAY AFTER PENTECOST/PROPER 28 55

These passages emerge from a world with a very specific set of expectations for the immediate future, world-shaking events climaxed by the return of Jesus Christ. How might we understand them in our own context?

As to 2 Thessalonians, there are undoubtedly churches, as there always have been, that are stirred up by busybodies: anyone who has given leadership to small town congregations, or even to some congregations in not-so-small towns, can testify to this. But it is difficult to conjure up a latter-day equivalent of the community assumed in 2 Thessalonians, in which an early expectation of the Second Coming will encourage idleness: nosiness, yes, and harsh judgments of others, certainly, but hardly idleness. On the other hand, there may well be circles of Christians today that need to be reminded to imitate Paul in his concern for the well-being of the brothers and sisters with whom he worked (2 Thess. 3:7-9). How church leaders today can help to shape the character of those whom they lead both by their urgings and by the convincingness of their own lives is a question indeed to ponder.

As to the Gospel, it is full of the specifics, as Luke has set them forth, of events to take place before the Jerusalem falls. Though these specifics were shaped by the actual horrors of the war of 68–70 C.E., Jesus had known perfectly well how people respond to wars and insurrections, to earthquakes, famines, and plagues; and he certainly understood well the kinds of challenge that his followers would be called upon to undergo before kings and governors. But Jesus was convinced that in a time of crisis the wars and persecutions, and the terror that these evoke in faithful people, were simply the birthpangs of the new world of God (see Matt. 24:8).

If, however, the first-century Christians were urged to relate the terrors of their day to a conviction of the imminent time of the end that would issue in the glory of God's new age, many present-day Christians have the opposite problem. We know that the present age did not come to an end in the first century, as those who heard 2 Thessalonians and Luke were expecting. The historical understanding of most of us, shaped by secular history, sees history moving on and on. We certainly witness terror-inspiring wars and insurrections, earthquakes, famines, and plagues, but for us these are events that tragically punctuate an endlessly extended sequence of centuries. And the fact that the wars and famines are mediated to us by secularized newspapers and television keeps our awareness of the hand of God at a distance.

Now of course there are some among us who do not buy into a secular understanding of history at all, but view the wars and insurrections, the earthquakes, plagues, and famines of our days as signs of the end time in precisely the way the first-century Christians did. But many of these folk view these signs in their own private conventicles rather than in the public arena. The Gospel, however, clearly envisages the events of the end, and the responses of Christians to these events, to be *public* ones, for all to see and hear.

So the question becomes: Is there any way to cultivate our own view of the richness of human history across the past twenty centuries but at the same time to see that richness as moving toward a culmination under the gracious hand of God? Verses 17-19 in the Gospel preserve the tradition that Jesus said, "Everyone will hate you for your allegiance to me. But not a hair of your head will be lost. By standing firm you will win yourselves life" (*Revised English Bible*). Is there any way to hear that great word as a reassurance in the context of the first century *and* the fifth, the sixteenth *and* the twentieth? Is God's end time perhaps richer and more variegated than a simple end to history at a datable point? Is there a way to hear in our own day, in all their power, the words of the Gospel, or the words of a passage like Rom. 8:38-39, "For I am convinced that neither death, nor life, nor angels, nor rulers, nor things present, nor things to come, nor powers, nor height, nor depth, nor anything else in all creation, will be able to separate us from the love of God in Christ Jesus our Lord"?

The present century is an ideal century in which to try.

Christ the King
Last Sunday after Pentecost
Last Sunday in Ordinary Time/Proper 29

Lectionary	First Lesson	Psalm	Second Lesson	Gospel
Revised Common	Jer. 23:1-6	Psalm 46 or Luke 1:68-79	Col. 1:11-20	Luke 23:33-43
Episcopal (BCP)	Jer. 23:1-6	Psalm 46	Col. 1:11-20	Luke 23:35-43 or Luke 19:29-38
Roman Catholic	2 Sam. 5:1-3	Ps. 122:1-5	Col. 1:12-20	Luke 23:35-43
Lutheran (LBW)	Jer. 23:2-6	Ps. 95:1-7a	Col. 1:13-20	Luke 23:35-43

Exegesis

FIRST LESSON: JEREMIAH 23:1-6

This passage from Jeremiah offers two short sequences, vv. 1-4 and 5-6. It is likely that both were proclaimed at the very end of Zedekiah's reign, just before the final fall of Jerusalem in 587 B.C.E.

The first sequence concerns "shepherds." This was a common designation for rulers throughout the ancient Near East; the image of God as shepherd is of course familiar to us from Psalm 23. Verses 1-4 are, curiously, both a judgment oracle and a salvation oracle at the same time. It is a judgment oracle against the "shepherds" who have misruled and scattered the "sheep" of Judah; it is at the same time a salvation oracle, since God declares, "I myself will gather the remnant of my flock out of all the lands where I have driven them" (v. 3). God takes over the task of shepherding, directly before the fulfillment of the promise to set up proper shepherds (v. 4).

Now when Israel was originally organized as the covenant people, they took it for granted that God would rule them directly: look at the affirmation of Gideon in Judg. 8:23. And even when the Israelites turned from this austere system and instituted the monarchy, it was still assumed that God was ultimately the ruler even though exercising rule through the mediation of human rulers. Jeremiah 23:1-4 thus affirms both God's direct and indirect rule.

In the second sequence, vv. 5-6, God promises in time to come a new king with the name "The Lord is our righteousness" (in Hebrew, *Yahweh-*

tzidqenu). This is a play on the name of the reigning king, Zedekiah (in Hebrew, *Tzidqiyyah*). Zedekiah had been put on the throne by Nebuchadnezzar and given that name—his name had originally been Mattaniah (2 Kings 24:17). Now the name "Zedekiah" could be understood to mean "Yahweh is [my] righteousness," but Jeremiah for his part doubted that Zedekiah had any idea what righteousness was. On the other hand, since the Hebrew word *tzedeq* can also mean "legitimacy" as well as "righteousness," the name "Zedekiah" could well be understood not as "Yahweh is [my] righteousness" but as "legitimacy of Yahweh"—indeed, it may well be that the name was chosen by the Babylonians (or by Judean advisors to the Babylonians) to reinforce the legitimacy of the man they had put on the throne. Since there were many folk in Judah who questioned Zedekiah's legitimacy, Jeremiah may well have had this issue in mind as well. In any event, by announcing a new king in time to come whose name reverses the elements of Zedekiah's name, Jeremiah is implying that while Zedekiah has the elements of kingship backwards (whether one thinks of righteousness or legitimacy or both), this new king, whom God will send, will get the elements of kingship right.

SECOND LESSON: COLOSSIANS 1:11-20

The authenticity of Colossians to Paul is a matter of debate: given the many contrasts in its phraseology from the letters everyone agrees to be genuine, a strong contingent of scholars today take Colossians to be post-Pauline, written perhaps between 70 and 80 by someone who knew the Pauline tradition.

Verses 11-14 of the reading are the last part of a sequence (namely, vv. 9-14) which embodies the content of the prayer that "Paul" offers on behalf of the recipients. Indeed, the whole of vv. 9-14 in Greek makes up a single sentence with dependent clauses and participles (compare these verses in the KJV). Recent translations, such as the NRSV, break these six verses up in various ways into separate sentences, and this approach allows the reading to begin with v. 11.

Verse 11 asks that the Christians at Colossae be strong to endure whatever comes, and vv. 12-14 enjoin them to give thanks that God has transferred them from the kingdom of darkness to the kingdom of light.

Commentators agree that vv. 15-20 embody a preexistent Christian hymn, though the beginning is somewhat masked in Greek, where v. 15 begins with the relative "who" (compare again the KJV). It has been suggested therefore that the original hymn had an opening line, like "Blessed be the Son of God," which v. 15 has omitted. The hymn breaks nicely into two strophes. Both begin in Greek with *hos estin*: v. 15, "he is [the image]," and v. 18b, "he is [the beginning]." Both continue with a causal clause ("for . . . ," in vv. 16 and 19), followed in turn in vv. 17 and 18 in Greek by a double "and he" (in the NRSV, "he himself" and "he is [the head]" respectively), and in v. 20 by "and through him."

The hymn proclaims the primacy of Christ in all things. He is the unique image of God, preexistent, before all creation; indeed, he created all things (vv. 15-17). He is head of the church (v. 18a), so that he has not only created all things but redeemed all things as well (vv. 18b-20). It would be hard to imagine rhetoric with more scope than this hymnic material.

GOSPEL: LUKE 23:33-43

This passage offers Luke's telling of the crucifixion. Verses 33-38 draw on Mark 15:22-32, though Luke has rearranged some of the material in that sequence of Mark's; furthermore, he has added the detail about the vinegar from Mark 15:36 and has added material from his special source as well.

It should be noted that v. 34a ("Then Jesus said, 'Father, forgive them; for they do not know what they are doing'"), though a precious part of the traditional passion narrative (it is the first of the so-called "seven last words of Christ"), is probably not original to the text. It is reminiscent of Stephen's prayer in Acts 7:60b, it interrupts the context in Luke, and it is omitted in many early and important manuscripts originating in a wide variety of locations.

The whole passage of Luke is of course appropriate to the festival of Christ the King because of the mention of the inscription over the crucified Christ, "This is the King of the Jews" (v. 38). Around this mention of the inscription are clustered three taunts, all of which mock Jesus, challenging him to save himself, and the second of which likewise mentions "King of the Jews." There is the taunt of the leaders, "He saved others; let him save himself if he is the Messiah of God, his chosen one!" (v. 35); that of the soldiers, "If you are the King of the Jews, save youself" (vv. 36-37); and that of one of the criminals hanging hearby, "Are you not the Messiah? Save yourself and us!" (v. 39). Since Jesus did not save himself from death, the taunts are ironic background to Luke's affirmation that Jesus is, after all, the one who saves.

Homiletical Interpretation

It is appropriate, after the lessons a week ago, which speak of the signs of the end time, to celebrate on this last Sunday of the church year the festival of Christ the King. Nevertheless, the lessons today, and the affirmation of Christ as "king," raise several issues for us. Two of these take our particular attention—the fuzziness that the word *king* conjures up in our minds, and the dissonance between the narrative of the crucifixion and the hymn in Colossians, with the related problem of the continued existence of evil in a world in which we proclaim Christ to be King.

Let us begin with the fuzziness associated with the word *king*. Kings are not as common as they used to be, and the kings that do exist today are either autocratic rulers who do not merit our respect, or else they are constitutional monarchs whose functions are largely ceremonial, symbolic of national unity. Mention "king," and we are likely to conjure up memories of Shakespearean plays or of faded photographs of the crowned heads of Europe gathering for the funeral of Queen Victoria. Furthermore, the very word *king*, connoting not only autocracy but *male* autocracy, is in poor repute in many circles. To bring anything very vivid and positive to the word *king* in our day then takes some work. Nevertheless, let us try.

The notion of "king" in the Bible has a complicated history, but Gideon's word in Judg. 8:23, already cited in the exegesis, is a good place to start. The Near East in Gideon's time was a world of kingdoms; indeed, our knowledge of the history of these states is often little more than a list of their kings. Gideon was a hero in turning back the Midianites, a tribe from the southeast who had raided the food supplies of the Israelites (Judg. 6:1-6). Indeed, he was such a success that there were Israelites who wanted to crown him king so that he could inaugurate a hereditary monarchy (Judg. 8:22). But Gideon refused; he held fast to the understanding of *covenant* set in motion by Moses. By this understanding, since Yahweh was the covenant God of Israel, and Israel was the covenant people of Yahweh, God thus took over the role of an earthly king. (Parenthetically, Gideon's son Abimelech evidently thought his father was a religious fanatic, because Abimelech was quite eager to let himself be proclaimed king—see Judg. 9:6; but Abimelech was killed by an unnamed woman, and thus that kingship did not last.)

This notion that Israel had was daring indeed, that they could withdraw their allegiance to any visible earthly king—indeed, dispense altogether with any earthly king—giving their allegiance instead to Yahweh, the invisible heavenly king. Yahweh was thus understood to carry out all the functions that any earthly king had, for example, seeing to social welfare and national defense (for these compare Deut. 28:3-5 and 6-7 respectively).

Nevertheless, in spite of Gideon and other true believers, this daring notion could not survive the various threats to Israel's well-being that came along—the internal threat of anarchy (Judg. 21:25) and the external threat of the Philistines. The Israelites then did institute a monarchy, beginning with Saul, and then with David and his descendants. Indeed, they preserved many testimonies that God had covenanted with David forever (see, for example, Nathan's oracle to David in 2 Sam. 7:8-17). But of course, as already indicated in the exegesis, the assumption was always that God, the heavenly king, was the sponsor of a given earthly king.

On the other hand, we must bear in mind that there were always voices that doubted that the turn to human monarchy was a good thing (see Hos. 8:4). So Jeremiah's mention of both divine and human kingship in the Old Testament lesson is fine evidence that there remained in Israel an ambivalence about the whole notion of human kingship.

But whether Israel understood God to rule directly or through human rulers, we cannot forget that the vision was of *governing*—effective governing, just and righteous governing. Here, then, is the nub of it when we deal with the symbol of "king": to see it as a viable and positive symbol for governing. And, one may add, when we use the metaphor of "king" for God (or for Jesus Christ), we are talking about the governing not only of our individual lives (as exemplified by the hymn "Take My Life, and Let It Be"), but also of our nations, our public institutions, our international corporations—of everything in our world that is.

The second issue is the astonishing cognitive dissonance between the hymn in Colossians, proclaiming Jesus Christ to be the creator and redeemer of all things, and the description of the crucifixion and death of that same Jesus Christ in the passage in Luke. We are so accustomed both to the theology of the passage in Colossians and to the story of the crucifixion that we are not likely to experience the dissonance as we need to.

For some perspective, then, let me refer to a very different figure from Jesus, namely the seventeenth-century figure Sabbetai Tzevi, whom Jewish history remembers as a preeminent "false Messiah." Sabbetai Tzevi grew up in Jerusalem three hundred and fifty years ago. As far as we can tell from descriptions of him, he was an attractive person, though he may well have suffered from what is today called a bipolar disorder (a manic-depressive condition). He certainly did not take the initiative in proclaiming himself to be the Messiah, but an associate named Nathan of Gaza did persuade him of this identity. Thereafter he moved around within the Turkish empire, eventually settling in Smyrna (the present-day Izmir, on the west coast of Turkey), where hundreds of Jewish followers gathered around him. News of his messiahship spread to Europe, and many Jews there sold their goods to make their way to Palestine for the inauguration of the messianic kingdom. There are testimonies that in the hall in Smyrna where a great feast was taking place, the prophet Elijah was seen to appear in the midst of Sabbetai Tzevi and his followers. Eventually the Turkish sultan, in Constantinople, summoned him, partly, it would appear, out of curiosity, and partly to keep an eye on a person with such potential to disrupt public order. Sabbatai Tzevi, for his part, was delighted to have the opportunity to present his messianic claims to the sultan, in whose territory Palestine lay—after all, the Messiah will soon replace the sultan! Eventually the sultan put him under house arrest.

Then, to the astonishment of his followers, he converted and became a Muslim. Many Jews, at this turn of events, abandoned him, of course, but some clung to belief in him all the more, for, they thought, is not the messianic kingdom a time when all norms are abrogated and Torah will be transformed? Soon after his conversion he died, and he was buried somewhere in what is now Albania; and though orthodox Judaism utterly repudiated him, nevertheless there remained small communities that continued to proclaim the messiahship of Sabbetai Tzevi well into our own century.

I offer this digression to put the messiahship of Jesus into context. I suggest that to an utterly neutral observer (from Mars, say) the messiahship of Sabbetai Tzevi, marked at the end by house arrest under the sultan and by conversion to Islam, presents no more barriers to belief than the messiahship of Jesus, marked at the end by his execution as a threat to public order by the Roman procurator. Both men were Jews whose followers made messianic claims about them; the earthly fate of both of them contrast sharply with the cosmic claims their adherents made for them.

Now, of course, the earliest Christians had ways to deal with this contrast between the death of Jesus and the triumph that they claimed for him. We see it in the early hymn that Paul cites in Philippians 2: "he [Christ] emptied himself" (v. 7), "he humbled himself" (v. 8)—"therefore God also highly exalted him" (v. 9). Indeed, the Easter narrative is the story of how Christ's humiliation was a prelude to his triumph.

Nevertheless, the fact that we can proclaim in the hymn cited in Colossians the cosmic kingship of Christ does not mean that we should not at the same time ponder the shame inherent in Jesus' crucifixion, the mockery he

CHRIST THE KING/PROPER 29

endured, the constant references in the Lukan narrative to kingship that do not cohere with any notion of kingship that the world would recognize.

Christ is a King who governs in a way altogether unlike any other king we have known; he governs not only with justice and compassion, but in humility and shame as well. We recall Isa. 53:10: "Yet it was the will of the Lord to crush him with pain. . . . through him the will of the Lord shall prosper." It is the paradox of the gospel.

There are many of us, however, who, though attracted by the humble Jesus, nevertheless see no real evidence of his kingship in the world around us. In what way, we wonder, is he King in a world of abuse of women and children, a world of ethnic cleansings, of nuclear threats, of ecological disasters? We can place our hopes in a final culmination of all things: in the Nicene Creed we say, "He will come again in glory, to judge the living and the dead, and his kingdom will have no end." Good. But the hymn in Colossians says, "In him all things hold together" (v. 17), present tense; where in the world in which we now live do we find all things cohering in Christ?

For some Christians the problem is not acute. Within their congregations and in the lives that they live they know the kingship of Christ; Christ is the Lord of their hearts, he governs their days and their years, and they await his final triumph in the world outside, when all things will be made right.

But this solution is hardly adequate to the issue, if Christ is King over all things now. The analogy proposed some years ago by the New Testament scholar Oscar Cullmann (in his work *Christ and Time*) is attractive. Christ's coming into the world and his present rule, Cullmann suggests, is something like the landing by the Allied Forces on the Normandy beaches on D-Day during World War II. D-Day was the crucial turn of events that made the Allied victory inevitable. Of course, after D-Day many battles had still to be fought, and many lives would continue to be lost, but victory was at any rate assured. So with the kingship of Christ: he has come, he has assured us of the final victory, we may give our allegiance to him in full confidence that the mopping-up operations that we see around us only bring us closer to the final triumph over all the forces of darkness.

The problem of the existence of the forces of darkness is acute. Even children wonder. Years ago, when one of my daughters was about four years old, she asked, "Daddy, why did God make big bad wolves?" It is a basic problem for those of us who shape our lives by the Bible.

And the Bible does not answer my daughter's question; what it does, however, is offer a vision of how the evil in the world is overcome. Let us survey the whole story, then. We begin with Moses' vision of the kingship of God to replace any earthly kingship, and this vision was compelling to Israel for many decades. Then human kingship, notably the dynasty of David, came upon the scene. And then, in the fullness of time, Jesus came on the scene, proclaiming the kingdom of God (that is to say, the kingship of God), just as Moses had, a kingship that was inaugurated by his own coming. His followers proclaimed him to be the Son of David promised of old, the Messiah to bring in the new age. He is a human king, as David was, yet, understood as the Second Person of the Trinity, he is the divine King as well. As both human king and divine King he thus fulfills both portions of Jer. 23:1-4, and indeed he fulfills vv. 5-6 of that passage as well, the king to come who merits the name "the Lord is our righteousness."

It is an awesome claim.